Fay Zwicky

POEMS 1970–1992

Born in Melbourne in 1933, Fay Zwicky began publishing poetry and short stories as an undergraduate at Melbourne University. She has been a concert pianist and was a Senior Lecturer in English literature at the University of Western Australia. She now devotes her time entirely to writing.

Widely published, Fay Zwicky's poetry appears in journals and anthologies both here and abroad. Her second volume, *Kaddish & Other Poems*, won the NSW Premier's Award for Poetry in 1982. Her next poetry book, *Ask Me*, received the W.A. Premier's Award for poetry in 1991 and was shortlisted in both the Victorian and NSW Premiers' Awards. *The Lyre in the Pawnshop*, a collection of essays, won the W.A. Literary Award for Nonfiction in 1987.

Fay Zwicky

POEMS 1970–1992

University of Queensland Press

First published 1993 by University of Queensland Press
Box 42, St Lucia, Queensland, Australia

Typeset by University of Queensland Press
Printed in Australia by McPherson's Printing Group, Victoria

Distributed in the USA and Canada by
International Specialized Book Services, Inc.,
5602 N.E. Hassalo Street, Portland, Oregon 97213-3640

 Publication of this title was
assisted by the Australia
Council, the Federal Government's
arts funding and advisory body

Cataloguing in Publication Data
National Library of Australia

Zwicky, Fay, 1933-   .
  Poems 1970-1992.
  I. Title.

A821.3

ISBN 0 7022 2466 9

to Karl and Anna
and the memory of
their father, K.T.Z., 1926-1985

Contents

**from *Kaddish and Other Poems*
1982**

New and Uncollected Poems

Isaac Babel's Fiddle

Perspective

1954:
There were the hours we spent
In gentle wonderment, walking together.
Shadows of the afternoon across our path,
Yet we were blinded by a greater sun, made
One and still divided in burning clarity of
Self, souls suspended in the bright air.
We were grave lovers, engulfed as by a mighty
Swell of tears; the pressure of the hand, the
Tender eyes, the whole merged in a whole, yet
You could speak — I was afraid to yield the
Vastness to a word, a sign that might trouble
The hour, the brightness and the joy.
We were grave lovers (you promised this would be
Although I doubted); our laughter grew
To a brave thing. So rare a day as this
We did not know would end so soon whose
Night was but the ashes of our noon.

1974:
I am supposed to blench for you, my heightened
Friend who loved. Miss R. who showed (said Bernard
C., whoever he) "cold purity of passion" but
"Added neither weight nor roused new hope thereby
For undergraduate poetry." He knew his stuff.
He knew that "burning clarity of self" was just
A blind, that wholes cannot grammatically or
Any other way be merged in wholes, that the
Existence of a soul was doubtful (Donne be damned)
In Melbourne of the Fifties. But calloused to
Survive, though he she loved is dead and she was
In another country burning laid, I wouldn't change
A word, young fuzzy platonist, whose fine illusory
Clarity throughout less heightened years has unmade
Me.

3

Survival Kit

I have waited to be forty all my life (always a
Sucker for precise reckoning), and
Here is the year beckoning me
To be where I always wanted, legitimately.
Dieu et mon droit, a confirmation devoutly
Wished for, a mark on the census that I am beginning
Where I began, that nothing has been worth winning,
That nothing has definitely been won,
Or absolutely lost.
        Heart's death old hat,
Mine has died time and again tending experience,
Absurd handmaiden to the absurd, removing my glasses
At movies, chickening on violence even at one remove,
Moping with Mahler, weak for my children, lead
Bleater of *Kindertotenlieder*, forestalling world's
End on the end of a pin, fraught with quibble and
Linguistic tic, pernickety ironic nit-picking
Academic.
        Bound to admit that I
Welcome the end of a world that I am, I rejoice
In the worm drinking dew, the lift as the leaf
Bursts its bud, gaiety in grief.
        Attitudes crumble.
The heart survives in bumbling triumphal shouts and
Giggles — in night skies, in the babble of birds,
Grass murmurs, bravura of rocks. So who mourns
Despair, anguish, fury, passion, fallen away
Painlessly as another year's petals? Did the
Nightingales carrying on in the woods of Mycenae
Give a damn for Agamemnon?

An Australian

(Self-Portrait by Clifton Pugh)

Before you buy your ticket, loose the
Atrophy of caste (white, skilled, and for
Ten quid you can, you can burn the pianola,
Galoshes, mum, and that inner man she hangs
About with) before I say, look well at this
Visible man, his holy frugal ghost.
They keep strange company. Poised between
Camps, you think he's free to pitch and fend,
Speculate and prophesy. You're wrong. He keeps
His end up by a tight-rope walker's trick,
Erectile stance, trial upon trial of fine
Adjustment in the austere shell of his curls,
Fronted by fall upon fall, a trunkless
John the Baptist, spectacled. Wordless
In a dumb landscape, sardonic, fretful, nurses
A faulty prospect without complaint.
Centaur in collage, below the belt he keeps
A flaccid rooted poise, knocks romantic cliché
In his groin-rumpled shorts, granite legs; clenched
Granite hand guards dying energies.
         Spectre to himself, the cloudless
Sky, the casual rocks, the sated sun, the broken camp;
Now are you game to plant your belly in that sun?

To a Sea-Horse

The male has a pouch on the underside of the tail into which the female injects the eggs. When the eggs hatch it looks as if the male is giving birth to the young. Even after hatching, the young remain near the father, darting back into his pouch if danger threatens.

Wall-eyed snouter, sweet feeble translucent
Tiny eunuch teetering on your rocker,
Pouting, corseted in
Rings of bone, flesh flaps
Fanning the tides as you totter and roll
Forward, but never so forward as
She.
Flex your pipes for the winter.
Keep an upright house.
Pucker piped lips for her, flex,
Flex your rings, flash your fin
If you can, man. Watch it!
Your love's bearing down with
Transparent efficiency, that
Abrasive lady's been starching her
Dorsal for meeting, nudges
Neatly your ring-tailed poise;
Totter and flex, finny vibrato for
Sex (can't afford to go off your
Rocker at this stage),
FLEX!
Chess knights collide:
A shuddering pouchful of eggs.
Nuzzle your snouters, sweet
Sons and daughters, tip to
Your tiny transparencies,
Hatched in your warmth,
Flexed in your strength.
They'd be mad to trust women
After this.

Isaac Babel's Fiddle Reaches the Indian Ocean

"Mr Zagursky ran a factory of infant prodigies, a factory of Jewish dwarfs in lace collars and patent-leather pumps. He hunted them out in the slums of Moldavanka, in the evil-smelling courtyards of the Old Market...My father decided that I should emulate them...I was fettered to the instruments of my torture, and dragged them about with me...One day I left home laden like a beast of burden with violin-case, violin music, and twelve roubles in cash — payment for a month's tuition. I was going along Nezhin Street; to get to Zagursky's I should have turned into Dvoryanskaya but instead of that I...found myself at the harbour...So began my liberation."

Isaac Babel — *Awakening*

Just try and cast a piano
In the sea
Romantically.
Take it from me, you'll
Never make it.

I tried it once
Or twice. My
Polished albatross
Kicked me as we
Sank through
Coral gardens.

And rose, rosewood
Bird and I,
Buoyed by
Bubbling spirals past
The emerald gills,
The darting purple fins,

Up through the silent
Gardens beckoning
In dappled solar tracks
To break the
Limpid bounds of an
Elysium aquamarine.

What happened when you left
That day? A day of frozen
Lakes and weighted birches,
Fleeing mittenless
The fond solicitude
That sealed your case

And thrust you talentless
Upon Zagursky's stoop to
Sit among the drooping
Ugly boys, your eyes
Intent upon their
Bruised necks, their neat

Doll's feet; Anchises' tadpoles
In withered velvet suits
Bearing their father, *theotokoi*,
Upon their bows to
101st street, East, the
Summerhearted phoenix land.

You'd seen your father
Touch his cap and bow
While Cossacks tore
His store apart.
Meanwhile your heart
Quickened with Dumas,

Stopped with Turgenev
(Disguised by Sevčik
On the stand). It was your
Judashand that flung the
Fiddle, spent the rouble
For Zagursky's care into

Odessa's sandbar — whose voice
Did you obey that day you
Sounded out the waterfront?

Hydrophobic shoot of land-locked
Scholars, febrile storekeepers
And gaunt Iberian rabbis in their caves.

The milling port that
Catapulted Heifetz, Elman
From the Tsarevitch's sight
Kept you, boy and man apart,
Heir to a single
Season of the heart.

You had no need to join
A brutal company;
(The world's a cossack haunt
In any case — Turgenev
Might have told you *that*),
What did you prove,

Master of silence? That you
Could pass the test
Your father failed, autumnal friend?
The silent salty wastes
Await us. These will
Get us in the end — meantime

The tendrils of the sea
Most tenderly embrace the
Adamantine gloss,
Time's rivulets are filtered,
Harmless, through each curled eyelet,
Every key is stilled.

The final feathered clamp
And suck of blind anemones
Rock the ancestral fate to jar
A host of ghostly swimmers,
Measuring their buoyant gravity
Beyond Odessa's black sandbar.

In Memory of Ries Mulder 1909–1973

Seeing the coming storm, tired of the way,
You drew to sleep. Rest quiet, Ries, who
Painted, talked, was loved by friends who
Fled the north and cannot bury you.
Blood in a lung, the new admitted guest
Sat in your room till we had gone, to
Swell his nightmare sac. An easy tender
Host, you gave yourself in gently
Angled prow suspended on an opalescent
Calm, painted when we were young
In Java.
How still it was. The red sun sank
Behind the spire, fired the canal and
Died. We drank to our next meeting,
Raised a glass against your subtle
Patient guest and ours. The sun's shaft
Struck the prow, shattered the summer
Waterscape one fiery time and charged a
Common autumn day with fear. You knew.
We set our faces light with expectation
(Time on our side, young in the south)
On a meeting: "Seven years? Of course
We'll make it."
Dear failed and gifted friend, the wind
Has blown us all to the earth's end never
To cross that sea again.
But on the clear cerulean wave your
Young and steadfast prow will rock
Itself asleep for ever.

Ijsselstein

10

For Anna

This is your friendly pelican
Talking to you, just above your ear:
The seas all rush together
As you chomp and snort among
My feathers. Burrow your
Pulsating skull against me,
Scan your larder well and choose
Your fill today, dear small predator,
Scrabbling to be free. Tomorrow,
With your trusting breath and
Reckless gums you shall devour
The world. And me.

Orpheus

As at a sign you'll go and no more
Turn. Night's window starred with warning
Runway markers opens: the plane waits.
Solemn boy again, I took your case with
Love, pity — books, you said, just books,
The squirrel hoard, the refuge, chosen
Cage. Our light affectionate irony
Played between the bars deceiving none
But us. Trapped migratory birds
More reckless of their years would
Probe a prison no more gentle — their
Simple islands lie in the sun and
Do not move. Our quicksand havens shift
To outstay the gnawing tides of love.

The Name of the Game

John Donne, who are you kidding?
"...nor yet canst thou kill me."
            Fine words.
Ah, fine fine words to gird the heart,
To brush me for a minute to infinity.
But back I come. And so did you, be
Honest now.
            Each night
I tell him in the sink, tell him
Scouring the floor on his black back:
Get the hell out of my kitchen!
I'm not ready for you yet and
When I am I'll do the taking.
Fine literary stance, poor heir to
Papa Ernest (poorer comforter than you).
But at the small pale root
That bound me long before I read a book
A swelling starts, a dark flower
Opens waxen leaves — no poppy this,
Dear John Chrysostomos.
            The voice of wax
Tells me the taker's name
And I (and you) believe it.

Respite

Ay, many flowering islands lie
In the waters of wide Agony.
— Shelley

Skeined and scented shore,
Spray drifts in piney whiffs
Suspended in sunlight.

Our moon-light thongs skim
The monotonous delicacy
Of skeletal shells,

Shallow fragile island
Sand, you on Rottnest,
I in Hydra. *"Hudra"*,

Corrects Nick the God giving
My son a short back-and-sides
In Nedlands, assimilating him

Head first into the land
of short back-and-sides,
Paving his track while I'm

Away on Hydra: *you* are
Always where you are,
Easy heir to lake and mountain

Bleak with guilt and tamed
By God. And on this guiltless
Strand you too are guiltless:

Unpilgrim'd fragile earth,
Where is my absolution?
Comical wife in a pink hat

Looking for what? A world
In a grain of sand when a
Grain of sand is a grain

Of sand (so they tell me
In this straitened land:
His name *is* Theos, I didn't invent

Him, and he has a son,
An Aristotle or a Plato, also
With short back-and-sides).

"Hudra has no cars, many tourists;
No, I have no wish to return.
Not yet." When his and my son

Greet the scented sand
Will they touch Rottnest or
Must my shoot propitiate

The Hydran gods for ever?
Have crisp white minutes
In a Nedlands barber's chair

Refused to chill the
Chafing ghost? Yet drowned
Beneath the turquoise-purple

Bowl of bay, lashed
With fine white streamers,
Stroked with sunlight,

Cruelly triumphantly unshriven
I am spent in you, the gods no more
Than distant thunder at a feast.

The Gift

Today I thought she gave me
Back the eyes I'd lost,
Contained and tough, painted
An elephant, trunk
Ecstatically reared,
Feet set fast

In a field of spiky grasses
Trees. Above, birds of red,
Green, purple and orange hang
In fine suspense. Equidistant
Careless and serene they loop
A tranquil sky.

Primed by his clenched unshaking
Creator, the earless beast
Bellows her triumph to the stars.
Quickened, I'm thrust to earth,
Pulsed by the ebbing riot of
My child's making.

Emily Dickinson Judges the Bread Division at the Amherst Cattle Show, 1858

I Volume

Here is bread:
  not more nor less than what you see,
It asks for mercy — I am God to give —
Stands as I stand (armoured, gleaming white
Behind my muslin smile, grand upon
The sweetness of this fearful day),
Waits on my step, my virgin adversary, life
Unflinching whole, upon a weathered bench
Pleading a tiny pellet of justice.
Of *me*!
    Reaper or victim, so far the act is fine;
Pastor Jenkins' nose approves my draped humility
But cannot smell my pride — I shine
Upon his coat behind a smile.
Yes, there is Bread:
    and I am where I am,
Winged, decorous, stony-hearted captive judge;
Nobody dare befriend me.

II Texture

Moonscape sways, the crested craters yawn
Under my knife, propitiating sabbath stroke:
    My father's economic vestal,
He would eat no bread but mine, contractor
For my crumb, his own communicant forever
Wrapped about a stone.
Votaries rebuffed resume, their crowns awry,
The silvered lacey cells; and God marks
Time, awaits the silken even grain.
    Today

Your starving eaglet breaks pitted bread
With sparrows — no question of friendship.
    But is't for this
I'll go, strangling in smiles, to heaven?
Mourn the eagle, mourn the sparrow,
Pastor can you? Test the crater's rim for me,
Shelter my responsibility beneath your
Tight black coat — here,
Here is the knife!
A healthy crust but I suspect
Surfeit of saleratus.

III Aroma

I cut, cut, cut,
My culprit dies in my wrath.
Wafted by bells on his winged collar
Rises, buoyed by sweet wraiths
Into fine new air.
    Strutting
In yeasty quicksands I send him at last,
About my neck the acid victor's wreath,
My smile stuck fast.
    Amherst's pigeons
Ponder the sourness in the air.

IV Colour

White is the colour of tribulation
White is the antimacassar of my cell
White is the inexorable collar
White is the dealer's hand
White the entrenched priestess.

Full marks.

Lear, Class '71

Trendy misses
In your gypsy dresses
Combing down your
Images of death,
Today's theme is
Renunciation:
Violets dwindle
On your breath,
Sunlight lilts upon
Your hair. *Look, will*
You a moment at the
Sequence of suffering…
Have you, Miss Hardcastle,
Another word for it?
Avoid it, then, by
All means — the
Rest of you
Take
Note.
Miss Hardcastle's father,
Bauxite magnate, knows
Never to give away:
(a) lands
(b) knights
(c) retainers for:
To be powerless
Invites
Attack.
He countenanced violence
In the nursery; Miss
Hardcastle orders her fear
With a moral, and young
Mr Middleton there, wandering
In the meadows of her hair
Yields to

Formal justice.
As they (and you) grow older
Your teachers will become
Somewhat evasive
On the subject, resort to
Delicate stratagems
To give the iron ball a miss,
To skip the rack, to pare
The teeth of:
Serpent
Vulture
Tiger
Bear
Wolf
Kite and,
Need I remind you,
Dog, coiled
In the obedient mind,
Images merely.
"Microcosm of the Human Race" —
Regrettable overstatement but
One suggestive of profound
Truth to be:
Defined
Analysed
Expanded
Qualified
For next
Week.
To suffer ripeness,
If it come,
Extends at present
Beyond the bounds of
Your curriculum and
The Administration
Chooses to
Grant us
No Extension.

Catullus at Sirmio

Time to speak well of the dead — who
Better than I, hunched on a
Rise in the delicate snows above
Garda whirling in crested froth.
My bleaching eye welcomes the skiff
Dancing to the whipping Dolomite blast
Between solemn pleasure boats,
Perfututa futata. They are coursing to
Riva, Malcesine, Desenzano chock with
Men, women like armchairs pink
Northerners frozen and stuffed, grasping
The coast pitched aghast from the
Curling steeps and hollows.
With reason.
Their owners are responsible men who
Threaten their captains regularly;
Perfututa futata, the asses are riding
Unpredictable waters.
I assure you that safety was never my
First consideration: my dervish sail
Rose to the crags of Dalmatia, the Cyclades
Hissing in oil to the violent Pontic, the
Lulling the lapping Pontic (O
Lesbia defututa futata!) and
O it is a cold day when pleasure
Hugs the dark coast.
      Giggling spirochetes twirl
Through the alleys of Rome, the lesbians,
Faggots, the whole jigging tribe of Clodii
Perfututa futata, I cooked them and ate
Them for supper agitating old stiffening
Cicero preparing his last case.

Spinoza's Lens

Baruch — ah, Benedict, best of both worlds and worst,
Who taught Elijah's chariot its place,
Squeezing the scriptural bubble until it burst

And shredded in the furred Sanhedrin's face.
Smart boy! He's learnt some names. Now he can talk
Of Descartes, Kepler, Galileo — words
As even his father can't pronounce. The chalk
Descends with violence: from the burning bush rise birds.

Fledged, forged, reviled
In this intemperate school,
Whose infinite indifference kept
Your buoyant pessimism cool?

Summer Pogrom

Spade-bearded Grandfather, squat Lenin
In the snows of Donna Buang.
Your bicycle a wiry crutch, nomadic homburg
Alien, black, correct. Beneath, the curt defiant
Filamented eye. Does it count the dead
Between the Cossack horses' legs in Kovno?

Those dead who sleep in me, me dry
In a garden veiled with myrtle and oleander,
Desert snows that powder memory's track
Scoured by burning winds from eastern rocks,
Flushing the lobes of mind,
Fat white dormant flowrets.

Aggressive under dappled shade, girl in a glove;
Collins street in autumn,
Mirage of clattering crowds: Why don't you speak English?
I don't understand, *I don't understand!*
Sei nicht so ein Dummerchen, nobody cares.
Not for you the upreared hooves of Nikolai,
Eat your icecream, Kleine, *may his soul rot,*
These are good days.

Flared candles; the gift of children; love,
Need fulfilled, a name it has to have — how else to feel?
A radiance in the garden, the Electrolux man chats,
Cosy spectre of the afternoon's decay.
My eye his eye, the snows of Kovno cover us.
Is that my son bloodied against Isaac the Baker's door?

The tepid river's edge, reeds creak, rats' nests fold and quiver,
My feet sink in sand; the children splash and call, sleek
Little satyrs diamond-eyed reined to summer's roundabout,
Hiding from me. Must I excavate you,
Agents of my death? Hushed snows are deep, the
Dead lie deep in me.

Song of Experience

The tasteful landau rolls its course
Discreetly grey, the pusher's wrist applies
The new-born knack, swoops on the curb to
Surge, primed with mysterious rites of
Fluent and felicitous resource.
Anchored upon his back the infant
Gravely sweeps the cushioned world,
Freckled by tender endless leaves, the
Crenellated mottlings of summer's breath;
Slyly unfurled, an eye describes the ageless
Promenade, imprints a lightning presence on the sky
And briefly renders down his graven death.

And Innocence?

The light spins out against your drowsy lids
Your craft is manned,
Pulsed by your dreaming halcyon heart,
By summer spanned

You roll. Though fretful tracings of the sun
Divert your sight
Your space probe purges earth
Of day and night.

Unwhorled, unpoled, unpressed to qualify
Your sleeping breath,
Your supine flight, inviolate stunt man, yet
Unbriefed for death.

Gall Tripartite

Heriger, bishop of Mainz, saw a prophet who said he had been carried off to hell. Among other details, he revealed that hell was surrounded by dense woods. To this, bishop Heriger replied with laughter: "In that case I'll send my swineherd to that grazing ground and get him to take my thin pigs with him."

From the MS of St Augustine

I Cold Ham for Sigmund

The clever cleric knows the rules,
A recognised authority
On all the grids and cul-de-sacs
Of limbo, hell and purgatory.

Good citizens of Mainz rejoice
That Heriger is in the chair!
If what you thought was hell today
He'll let you know it wasn't there

Tomorrow. Arch-rotarian, he will
Send his cheerful pigs to make
Reconnaissance, investigate
Infernal sprawl, pronounce it fake.

So keep it underneath your hat
If demons seize you by the hair,
For Mainz prefers its porkers fat
And heavenly fodder's everywhere.

II Look here, Vladimir...

You! European you, with the
Pained fastidious bones,
Take off your exclusive cross and hush

Your cheery omniscient groans.
What makes you suppose yourself to
Be so final an authority
On the stink of suffering's rose?

Do I have to wave an Auschwitz stump
To attest my fitness, *pour*
Mieux comprendre the
Pacific equine rump
Of Bosch, the wart
On the conjurer's nose?

III   *Plus Ça Change...*

Old Henry commiserates with Hedda,
(A rusted pistol rattles to the floor)
Manipulates as *beautifully* as ever
Seraphic permit to terrestrial door.
Both find that they have in them to agree
Upon the source of their infirmity.

The screw turns aimlessly into the silt,
Hélas, it only pricks a barren spring;
The coupled squeak with boredom from the quilt
Mechanically doing their own thing.
Observing simple pleasures never cloy,
Our pair retrieve their winding sheets with joy.

Totem and Taboo

I

Great grandpa Saqui set in sepia,
Wall-eyed pensive from a century's nap,
Lingers on an ancient book.
His blasted eyes brook dreaded distance,
Navigate between the darkened Liffey
And the clouded Melbourne stream,
My stem and tap-root trapped in pewter.
Mad Jew-Christ in a tipsy brougham
Rending O'Connell Street with exiled cries
Waving a long onyx at Torquemada's
Hibernian guard and I will go,
He said (mad he was, I repeat),
Go, and let you get on with
Your dirty business.

The Jew is constrained to flee the commotions of Ireland.

      En route he belted
Mendelssohn's spring song at Victoria
In her glass house, bowed and hurled himself
(Satrap second-class) headlong at her
Far-flung province, fortified with lemons
For the old sow held his mate in nets too
Taut for even his manic importunings;
And in the turquoise furrows drowned
The northern stars in furious tears.

Making course for the tropical Latitude of the Great Pacific, the Jew playeth upon the organ for Victoria Regina.

28

II

Claimant to Valhalla's ranks, he took
To horse, a bellicose black jewel to
Fly around the Saxon emerald fields,
Baring his teeth to mock the cocky
Bastard accent that had dared
To call him "Worrier". And hanging
At his beck and kick a beggar-king
On fiery stilts, Jew among Cossacks,
Bounding quisling to the prayerworn ghetto;
A pair of violent uncouth coat tails
Hot upon a nag's behind that arched
Its banner in his face and plopped the
Crumbling apples of contempt
Before his feet.

The Jew
purchaseth a
horse in
expectation of
salvation.

Careless of his masters, sparking off
A thousand fires the thundering jewel
Panicked some seagulls with a windy rush
And smote apologetic aeons on the nose,
Unsettling the wavering fringes of
An aged shawl.

'Warrior'
winneth the
Melbourne
Cup, 1865.

If small recrimination
Ever snubbed the edge of his recruitment
Nothing ever found a way to the old sow,
Glutted with her farrow (save a line
In graceful and bizarrely cautious
Arabesques of veined ink).

The Jew
findeth not
salvation; the
penance of life
falleth upon
him.

The Chosen — Kalgoorlie, 1894

I *The Escape*

His father said: Marry her. She's had a hard life —
With you lighter it can't get. She cooks,
Breathes, a little ankle, eyes not bad...what
More do you want? For mother's sake...
her heart won't beat for ever...a grandchild, a family!
And he ran away. He ran and ran from that
Abrasive calico breast, virgin ankle, awkward
Menial hands, his heart burdened with crimson sunsets.
(Grandmother-mother, hands that moulded love in me but
Passive lay in his impatient palms). Thin spectacled,
Sixteen he fled the fatherland across the Nullarbor.
His mother had her heart-attack and Yahweh,
Rhadamanthine Yahweh (blest be He!) galloped
Snorting after the little puffer. Bobtails blinked,
Smiling among grey stones to see
God go off His Head.

II *Retribution Plotted*

And Yahweh the Extravagant,
Prodigal Yahweh swore revenge,
Stamped in a desert way off His patch:
A Desert-Dweller all My life!
Don't they know of Me? The trumpet-tones
Shatter on flat stones; ant-hills heave,
Turn over in a dreamless sleep:
My Chosen do not stray far! My ways are wondrous,
Perilous; I am the One (no other shalt thou have)
Who does the choosing here!
Braying maniac brewing cataclysms.
Antediluvian mouths yawn
Under the unshriven sun.

III The Plague

They handed him a key:
This is your house. A sagging box,
Smoke-licked pane webbed by
Sleepy crab-spiders. He'd read
In the old country, Talmud-ridden
Fly, "In hot climates Spiders
Are able to produce a certain amount of
Local pain." His skin bristled with small
Spiked crowns. Pain's antidote in peeled
Tub — a pink geranium, stationmaster's ward,
Barren season's suckling.
Weekly his charge gnawed the track to the
Flat horizon, covered a hemisphere in his
Kindled sight, gabbling caterpillar.
But came the Day of the Scorpion.
Clanking, thundering scales, buckling linkages,
From its final poisoned segment issued Yahweh,
Mighty polyphemal ruby eye to sear the spider,
Flower and stripling stationmaster, belching
Plague through flaring nostrils, scattering
Dybbuks through the land.
I CHOOSE, HEIR TO ASHES! Squeaking demons,
Metal-winged, buzz and swoop, pegged within
The confines of His breath.
Ten days he lay reflected in his death, his
Bowels curled limp beside his shoes.
Next train his grieving father
Brought him home.

IV Retribution Achieved

She said: This is the station key.
Your grandfather watched trains as a young man.
I waited.

Forbearance — Coolgardie, 1898

He soon shall find Forbearance no acquittance

Aunt Phoebe spent her
Rocky middle years inside
A tent upon the goldfields,
Swore at tardy camel trains
And waterless, she rued the day
Of comfort's banishment.

Uncle Barney entertained the
Boys inside their tricorne —
Leathern Bacchus and his pards —
Together clashed the tin pan cymbals,
All agape they loafed around her, shrill
Fermenters of the messianic grape.

Aunt Phoebe gave short shrift to
Her messiah, bore her child and
Fanned her fire and wished
The day would come when hell
Should loose some extra flames
And sear the lot of 'em.

Meanwhile she irritably tried
To rear a plot of green outside
Her pitch, forgetful of her wish.
'Twas granted. The infernal powers
Revealed with one swift scorching puff
That grass roots seldom burrow deep enough.

Don Juan at the Record Bar

Glass-pure drops of sound hang
Fresh in the morning air.
Mozart and his death come
Face to face in the
Saturday supermarket.
      Put a
Requiem under your own roof!
You idly twirl the stand,
Finger speculates on sideburn
Styled by Mr Troy.
      Will you
Have it in mono? Stereo? Whatever
You decide we guarantee its
Positively final efficacy.
Look sideways at her long blue-frosted
Eye, alien frieze of narcissistic lust;
Come, you'll play with me, sir?
You strain, and drown. Your
Minted heads discuss the tone: you
Don't have this on stereo? Shame.
Amadeus rolls his chambermaid in
Bed of flame.
      Braced,
The Commendatore waits behind the door.

Chicken

Tucked snug behind
Proscenium arch a
Baby's stoned to death:
The watchers sit in trembling furs,
Slumped with relief.
Beyond belief!
Come, let's get out before
The peak hour traffic snarls
The bridge. I've got cold chicken
In the fridge for supper — at least
I think I have. Those kids *will*
Gorge themselves. Oh go on,
You can pass! The light's already
Amber, hurry up! I'm dying for a
Cup of tea. Don't talk like that
To me, of all people!
Let's not quarrel, things are
Going so well: Ian's done his maths
And Nigel's sure to top his year.
You've worked so hard with
Him…what's that? I
Had to keep her home. You
Know that stomach thing she gets.
She'll be all right tomorrow.
Well, the wings have had it but
The breast's still there. Or
Part of it. You must be starving!
Can't see why we push ourselves to
Plays like that although I feel
The writer has a point to make.
Some cake? Oh damn, I
Gave it to that child next door;
I'm sure her mother doesn't
Feed her properly. What's the

Matter? Aren't you feeling well?
It'll pass. There's Dexsal in the
Cupboard and a glass is
Right in front of you.
All right, I'll come up later —
What a mess they leave the
Place! Did you say she was crying?
Probably a dream. It's just a phase
She's going through. I'll go to her.
You go to bed. I can't think
What's the matter with my head.
        There, there, the
Way you cry you'd think I was an
Awful sight. Now be a good girl,
Go to sleep. Good night.

Scoop

Colombian vines, the jungle swirl of
First dank life have lapped his exile;
An Indian wife, a patch of corn and herbs
Beneath a fall of perpendicular gneiss.
The travellers stand amazed above the
Precipice, scan his scars, skin, seek to
Nail his public possibilities, prints of an
Old and private life blur beneath their
Lenses, scrupulous distinctions of revenge.

Hauptmann?
Ehrmann?
Bormann?
Hartmann?

Drum and flute repine among the swelling roots,
The stalking vines have leapt to cover
An old man confounded with detail, at one
With thieves and murderers of
Other places, other times.

A Midwestern Wife

After the funeral came the sons to paint
The house for her, but when the painting
Was half done they quit, leaving a twilit zone
For the remainder of her days.
                Widowed Lady of the
Moose, ex-Illinois Porkette, her Dewey dead at 45,
Farmed hogs, beans in Tuscola till they came shooting
Out of their ears, Veteran of World War I, Barracks 890,
Built a concrete basement, installed an oil furnace,
Left: a wife
    two sons, Elmer and Willard; one, Jim, died before he
      counted
    two daughters, Mrs Kathy Bormann and Mrs Holly Grabb,
      both
    of Mahomet, on the day Amy Schlorff's pet ostrich Herkimer
    ran amuck and outran in fact every man and boy in town. And
Also left:
    five grandchildren
    two sisters
    and a brother, Sonny, who preceded him in
    death, former gardener, groundskeeper and
    nurseryman at Appalachian Bible Institute, Tenn.
    and up to no good most times.
The widow taught school 40 years (junior English),
Was a charter member of the Tuscola 1st Baptist Church
Was a member of Sigma Iota Xi
Was a member of the National League of American Penwomen
And in addition was the author of *Homespun*, a book of
Poems, *Daily Lesson Plans in English*, and *The Cross of the
Redemption*. An exemplary life, season to season, said the
Pythian sisterhood knotting their tails. Smarter than old
Dewey at the best of times, scrambling boy.
That kind don't wear so well.

Guarded by successions of
Cantankerous dogs, the rats were kept out of the beans.
Weakening once, she wept briefly in the bean rows,
Stiffened, hired a large and surly boy to rake and
Mow on Saturdays. Death took friends, relations
One by one, perching on her window ledge waited
With blank tact.

   The parched flanks flaked in
Summer storms, dust whirled her round corners,
Spring ice seared the magenta-tipped magnolia,
Charred the fever-bright forsythia, slew her tulips.
Violets kindled like weeds. She tore them up,
Began to mumble a little, forget a little, shake
As her house shook uncontrollably in the cunning
Prairie winds that tracked her to her door.
Neighbouring children stole pears from her tree.
The hard old hand crumbled in the summer haze.

   And one day she saw that
Everything was grey, a day no different from any
Other day but she saw:

   Her house was grey
   The trees were grey
   Her hair, the words of her sons,
   Her daughters, all her grandchildren
   All were grey
   Streets, cars, shoes, coats, hats,
   Hogs, horses, cows, goats, squirrels,
   Rats, pigeons, doves, cats and all the dogs
   Were grey and above all the sky was wide
   Grey from the moment you opened your eyes
   And why did I never see it before,
   Why and what does it mean?

Nobody answered.
She didn't much expect an answer, certainly
Not from grandson Larry potting begonias in the
Back yard, no religion to speak of but not a bad boy,
Not bad at all . . .

   She moved to dark and shady places,

Lily-of-the-valley sprang unwanted, past her quince
Blossom, hulking crabapple, and the wild blue phlox.
In the dark waxen leaves rummaged sightless, deaf,
Dumb now, pulling at the toughened lily roots, tearing,
Scattering the threaded waste over the ashen mulch, the
Grey soil of her life.
There is no more to be done, and
Took the last bit in her stride.
                    There was no visitation by request.
Donations could be sent to the Blind and the Daughters of
Pythias huddled their crocodile tails against wailing
Prairie winds telling what a shame when she still had
So much go left in her but that's life and
When do we meet again?

Memorial Day & Tornado

Half a planet over they roar to Indianapolis
Flash-flooding cockpits of paternal memory.
Easy-on easy-off gum based shuffle kids trailing
Broad-bellied dust funnels off Interstate 74,
Exploding kegs and cans against tomorrow's corn.
Momentous issues have lost
Their moment. Old guards sobered, war being done,
Leave well alone.
      Today more distant Furies have declared
Us a disaster area. Irresistible, these coarse seductions
Of the truth, an apocalypse not more passionate than a
Bit of wind and water. We flare and fold in swift turns
Of national concern. The man who comes to read the meter,
Those flattened nasal body counts on Thursdays were
Steadier stuff.
Stocks hold in central Illinois. Centennials, awards
For oratory, homemakers of the month keep the keel
Temporarily even.
Fire brigades are there to put out the fires.
The shabby shifts and glitter of desire are blacked
As Over Death We Triumph.
      Quietly a semi-trailer rolls the
Nearby cornfield, slow dream-like rollover driver floats
To rest in a sea of Valvoline drums. Panicked by the
Suddenly huge black funnel snaking his screen, how small
He lies. His nightmare turns, slouches to Kansas, shrunken
To daytime size.
      Bugle taps thread pot-holed town to town,
Dim beads frost flat silence. Over death triumph the
Graven brotherhood, Knights of Pythias:

Ardrey Aescher
Bagby Bobowski
Clabaugh Coonz
Finkbiner Dye Eberspache Fieldbinder
Fijolek Filipek Finbloom Fleischmann
Gentilli Hasenauer Hagen Hoffmeister
Hapke Harness Harnsberger Heimburger
Holmblad Lovby
Machula Magyar
Maartens Meyer
Michie Redlich
Reifsteck Rich
Zepecki Zemlin
Zugenbuehl Zyc
From fresh-mown lanes, green as butchers' fern,
Spring little flags exploding, rearing, waving
Bright and dragonish today. As keen as yesterday
Had never been.

4-Lane Divided

With what intemperate sense of waste did they
Abuse the times, unwinding skeins of wind,
Grey streamers flagging their immense wake to
Soar in limbo flat and meaningless as Utah,
Kindly but firmly fenced away from time, days,
Hours of a country they were never easy in.
Moonman and family pierce a cold pane.
      Sun,
Luminous plum through mist, draws south the
Compassless armed with an ambiguously-worded
Proclamation of intergalactic trust.

There goes everybody, there goes nobody;
Men in short thunderbolts thud the measureless
Face of loneliness. Assured in motion span a
Continent like any old backyard, volleying
Towards home sense home.
Exile is to arrive.

Fungus Epidemic

Our coming was black in December, slow grey to
Black and back. Darkness followed darkness, night
Night. Smoothed out by shock we were stripped
Down efficiently for the new season, to be shown
To be divided.
       Wind reared dead life around,
Arranged in quick sharp blasts lines of wintering
Leaves and bone, ragged cot-cases for our inspection.
People keep saying how normal it all is. They have seen
Disease, the day all the elms in Urbana died overnight:
Stretched beside my husband I have been found unfit
For saying what kind of place is this to bring
Children to when what I really mean is I am frightened
By the smell, the corruption of death, the shouting
Tides of my death specifically, an old woman fallen
Out of space, unready.
       Flooded, I shake in the dark. My hands,
Encrusted with apple-scab, lame the stride of his dream.
I fumble to replace our fallen leaves.
       Dark still, and May. Seasons crawl.
Cracked crimson flowerheads bow to grass, whole
Yesterday. A tornado watch is out till midnight.
Terraced by fungus the sycamores strike at us.
Their sickness is clean, white, odorless. I am not
Disturbed by it. The circles of forgiveness have
Shrivelled a little with the year's passing.

Urbana, Illinois

The Garden of the F'u Dogs

Like loping indolent kings, the four of us process.
Survivors of a picnic, sausages and punch, the tidy
Swooping rituals of frisbees crimson, blue, and one
Rubber ball astray in a small fortuitous pond.

The earth is steady, the sun warm and shadowless.
Our subjects a little ungovernable — straggled paths,
Slopes of fern and bracken, wary grasshoppers but
Nothing charmed. Clean white birches, planes and
Hickory, a prodigality of grass and leaves that give
The sky no quarter, harbour no phoenix either.

Another family trails politely silent in our wake.
A little bored with nothing to dispense we move,
Reserve our largesse for the Garden of the F'u Dogs.
Taking stock of distance from a central oasis, one
Tall white rotunda flanked by bronze Buddhas in central
Illinois our step becomes more formal,
A pavane of abdicated will.
Gods of a kind are here. Down what seems a mile
Or more of green rectangular lawn hemmed by dark pines,
Expansive, claustrophobic both, we keep our distance.
They theirs. The heavy sinews of a coming storm flex,
Baffle the air grown tight around us. We move on,
Guarded by the rigidly spaced altars of the demon dogs,
Governing our little space with ancient glossy haunches,
Dark blue glazed and sated vigilance.

Allerton Park, Illinois

Little League

Daylight saved at seven for three fathers.
Two white, one black, planted thrusting in a
Field of immemorial caps, the snubby shapes
Of sons.
    Prairie winds drive back the sky
To let them run. Bat-flick. Legs.
Earth shifts beneath them, tremors shake
The world.
    "Run, Al! For your life, boy!"
The eternal cry. A dog, stirred by ancient
Memory, pees against the new-leafed birch.
Bark slivers, fine as burnt skin, shake in
The wind.
    Urged by grey-green phantoms, shapes
Of older brothers drawn from Hanoi
Phosphorus and flame to cheer, they hit and
Run as innocence drums in another
Shivering season.

Dogwood

Vanished in winter, trackless. Unwithered waits
Her fierce festival. Prowls the brush a season
To rear again a tainted ivory perfection and
Devour the sky.
      She has a reputation, this stagey
Unwearied predator, catches cue from an
Intimidated modest cast still raw,
Aghast from snows and winds of Canada.
Silence everybody.
Unrolls a deafening bold corrupted breadth
Of petal. On one swift measured beat
Accents her masterful flesh.
Layer upon layer, shadowed space mimics
Each creamed muscular perforation.
The sheenless green unseeing eyes
Acknowledge nothing.
      Idolatrous packs press to hold
The perfect prey, stripper of infinite promiscuity.
With one ample move eludes the quest, vanishes
Shameless and unwithered.
      Crenellated images prick out
In fevered paper constellations minds
That know beauty when
They see it.

Leaving Chicago in December

Driven in upon themselves like old men's eyes
They stare from corners. Not at us.
Children ballooning out of doors stamp
Into black rain.
    Maimed metal struts the grey
Green river ice, chips and stunted floes hold
The wind in swollen poison currents.
Black stars drive silent snow of an iron city.
Chicago, fretted furnace of old Indian night.
    Tensed, the bus breasts feckless
Blackened drifts. We stare, my children and I,
Through tinted glass at nameless people bound
To our nameless days.
    Bridling currents of estrangement
Twitch and well between us.

Republican Attorney & Client

Steel-rimmed Chancey Finfrock towers
Above Virgil Liptrap.
    Squinting at the
Main street giant, Virgil peers, sinks
Into the whale's maw of Chancey's shadow.
    His piping drone flares,
Dies, as Chancey's friendly teeth clamp shut
A none too promising case.

Waking

My young sister last egg of all thought
She safely black enough to mimic ethnic
Affliction, cried Lawd have mercy
Spare mah soul, hallelujahed allover
The house (a musical family) paining
Me, a prickish twelve, no jew nor black
Neither but whiter than Persil.

And the Lord let her caper, smiled on
Childhood dreamtime, me forgave not, bent
Himself double to push pride, ambition,
*Rugos' inflavit pellem,** flushed my greedy
Pellets down the wind till fit to puzzle
Pieces back, praised Him, woke
Monochromatic, pointed as Kafka.

* "it (the frog) inflated its wrinkled skin" — from Aesop's fable, "The Frog and the Ox"

The Prodigy Ages

Creation of pitch,
Perfect capering child with
Your stony heart and your
Decorous ear, buttoned in
Silence, your
Spirit disjunct.

Creature of atrophy,
Rosewood and ivory, fuming
Pique dame doubled over a
Limp pavane, waterproof
Celebrant of
Infant defunct.

Lot's Wife (Take 18)

Put in a word for life
She said.
Life who needs it who's
Making the scene anyway
He said so
Stuff yr. dissonant
Track yr. humdrum unlit
Undubbed wide-screen
Sepia footage and
Pass the salt
He said.
She did.
Passed herself
On a plate
She did.
That's life
She said
She did.

Projection Box

Art? said
The Poet
Let the
Head-on
Intimacy
Of my nerrrrr
                v
                 o
                  u
                   s
                 s
                 y
                 s
                  t
                   e
                    m be
My Impact. Anything
So naked
And o
       v
        e
         r
          w
           h
            e
             l
              m
               i
                n
                 g
Cannot fail
To move

Paperbacks

(with apologies to Kingsley Amis)

Snagged between *Fretwork for Beginners* and
1000 Hints for Handymen, the Poetry.
      Discriminating, idle for a day
I attend the Contents, soothing page — no one
I know, no one my age. Strangers sorted,
Focused by sex, *View of a Pig* — clearly a
Man. *Helen's Rape* — what else but?
Never woman's heroine ("She always had it
Coming to her," said the aunts of
Menelaus, "No pride, that's her trouble.")
Requiem for Plantagenet Kings? Who but a
Male would so squirm? Female madness
Assumes more desperate form.
Titles plead literacy: ("I contemplate," "I count
For something", "So you think *you* can scan",
"Not for nothing did I read Classics, major
In History" they shout at me.
But *Bedtime Story for my Son, Childless
Woman, The Abortion, Her Kind*, throw me
A minute. As in most affairs of the heart a
Moral smoulders in it.
      One must confess, despite
Contrary medical evidence (a Johns Hopkins
Psychologist no less) to a difference,
No matter the thousand mature female
Rats caged with the newborn; who needs
A rat? Menstruation, gestation, lactation
Haven't the dash of impregnation, but
Culturally determined? Optional?
      Poets tell more than most,
Inflate the heart or pulp it.
Men order such things; women just can't help it.
Enough never enough, the whole hog rendered from
Birth to conception to birth. Man diverts with

Nicely weighed perception, unseemly
(or so women seem to think) mirth.
           Small wonder that men then
Like women, envy them even, dimly recalling roosting
Long into the night, high in a star-pricked heaven,
Powerless to write.

Maharishi Consolator

The guru giggles on his pinnacle;
Plumply potted *Monsterae* adore
The throne. Upon the vinyl chairs
Of the Potala creased by
Celebrated students of the
Truth, a hush
Descends.
God has arrived at the
Appropriate hour.
The arms of Shiva Nataraja flail
The sticky air; east in wary
Truce with west shows lively teeth:
"We are, have always been, a
Spiritual people..."
The shrine approves the thought.
Respectful whispers glide between
The crenellated plastic floribunda:
"And so it is repeated in the
Fourth Brahmana a lonely person
Has desire of comfort..."
Epauletted bellhop hands the deity
A winking glass of frosted pineapple:
"Like you, we thirst..."
Sly frangipani dances at his
Ear, the point is fondled, held
Aloft... *"who is indifferent to honour*
And dishonour, to whom things sweet and
Things not sweet are equal, then is
He said to supervene the Moods; fivefold
Is this man, fivefold all this
Whatsoever. It is, indubitably,
So. You must believe; I bring
This message from Tibetan peaks." An
Elevator hums its way to earth, the

Waiter's eye flicks round — jeez,
What a bunch of freaks . . . *"Now
Do you have some questions
For me? After life you said
Kind gentleman?"* The master makes
A non-commital *moue* and shakes his
Head: *"Truly the Person is
Imperishable. Let man breathe up
And let him downward breathe that
Evil death may not attain
To him. And I say thus, and only
So shall he obtain a oneness, union
With his god..."*
            Hey,
Calm down, lady. Get him *outa* here!
Enough's enough; our staff is only
Trained to handle perishable
Stuff.

                                    Honolulu, 1968

Charity Ball

The demon drink conducts a
Blitz, the classes merge,
A waiter's eye flicks round —
The scions surge towards a
Waitress who retreats and packs
Herself against the festive meats.

Stamping their whiskied image on the
Joint, starched to the gills they
Itch, laced inside black shells;
Thrusting claws tighten a raffish grip
On ocean bed awash with crême de
Menthe and gin, they slip

Towards the evening's end, everybody's
Enemy, everybody's friend. Lift glass penultimate
To national service, old school ties, to widows
Spry in lavender. Pickled with glaucous zest
Concede of all the shows sweet charity
Puts on the best.

Campus Fable

"Seek Wisdom" sang
The fulsome swan
And floated to an
Easeful death. The
Cognoscenti took him
At his word and
Sought.

Meanwhile the bird,
Holed up at Lethe's
Wharf, had changed
His tune, enlightened
By his splendid final
Breath:

"A pity. If I
Had known what wisdom
Comes with dying, I
Might have spared them
Centuries of
Trying."

His poignant revelation
Passed unheard, and
Seeking still
They waned,
Conned by a
Bird.

Tea Room

Terra Australis, great dumb blonde
And vegetable whore, why did you let
Those righteous AS. bastards roll
All over your fruits? Better the
Wrought-iron Spaniard or
Black Portugee than all the
Civil trousered builders
Of society.

Had those lonely lazy hips
Plumped for swarthier memorials,
We might not now be hemmed with
Tea and eyebrows, wary aqueducts
Altered to Rome's foe, the slack
Unpolitic admission of two somewhat
Mediocre tutorials.

Literary Board

No one I know. No one my age.
The room — well, looms. On stage
Sit poets and historians, here
Today on behalf of and will be,
Maybe not. Don't ask lest it be
Granted. Kingdoms come and come
Again, dispatch their cultural
Emissaries in hair and snappy
Ties. Black brisk briefcases
Contain what must be contained:
The state of the state of our
Imaginative life, need for new
Forms (vital, meaningful) to
Nail apocalypses on the western
Front. All's still, the room too
Hot and science has once more
Failed: fans don't work, doubts
Are expressed for the future of
Poetry, concern for the ailing
Novel without a thorough knowledge
Of aerodynamics but if anyone
Really wants to he's welcome
To try that switch —

Kaddish
and Other Poems

Kaddish

For my Father
born 1903, died at sea, 1967

Lord of the divided, heal!

Father, old ocean's skull making storm calm and the waves
to sleep,
Visits his first-born, humming in dreams, hiding the pearls
that were
Behind *Argus*, defunct Melbourne rag. The wireless shouts
declarations of

War. "Father," says the first-born first time around (and nine
years dead),
Weeping incurable for all his hidden skills. His country's
Medical Journal
Laid him out amid Sigmoid Volvulus, Light on Gastric
Problems, Health Services

For Young Children Yesterday Today and Tomorrow which is
now and now and now and
Never spoke his name which is Father a war having
happened between her birth, his
Death: Yisborach, v'yistabach, v'yispoar, v'yisroman,
v'yisnaseh — Hitler is

Dead. The Japanese are different. Let us talk of now. The
war is ended.
Strangers found you first. Bearing love back, your first-born
bears their praise
Into the sun-filled room, hospitals you tended, city roofs and
yards, ethereal rumours.

Gray's Inn Road, Golden Square, St George's, Birmingham,
Vienna's General, the

Ancient Alfred in Commercial Road where, tearing paper in controlled strips, your
First-born waited restless and autistic, shredding life, lives, ours. "Have to
See a patient. Wait for me," healing knife ready as the first-born, girt to kill,
Waited, echoes of letters from Darwin, Borneo, Moratai, Brunei ("We thought him

Dead but the little Jap sat up with gun in hand and took a shot at us",) the heat

A pressing fist, swamps, insect life ("A wonderful war" said his wife who also
Waited) but wait for me wait understand O wait between the lines unread.
Your first-born did not. Tested instead the knife's weight.

* * *

Let in the strangers first: "Apart from his high degree of medical skill he
Possessed warmth" (enough to make broken grass live? rock burst into flower?
Then why was your first-born cold?) But listen again: "It was impossible for

Him to be rude, rough, abrupt." Shy virgin bearing gifts to the proud first and
Only born wife, black virgin mother. Night must have come terrible to such a
Kingdom. All lampless creatures sighing in their beds, stones wailing as the

Mated flew apart in sorrow. Near, apart, fluttered, fell apart as feathered
Hopes trembled to earth shaken from the boughs of heaven. By day the heart

Was silent, shook in its box of bone, alone fathered three
black dancing imps,

The wicked, the wise and the simple to jump in the house
that Jack built: This
Is the priest all shaven and shorn who married the man all
tattered and torn
Who kissed the maiden all forlorn who slaughtered the ox
who drank the water

Who put out the fire who burnt the staff who smote the dog
who bit the cat who
Ate the kid my father bought from the angel of death: "Never
heard to complain,
Response to inquiry about his health invariably brought a
retort causing laughter."

Laughter in the shadow of the fountain, laughter in the
dying fire, laughter
Shaking in the box of bone, laughter fastened in the silent
night, laughter
While the children danced from room to room in the empty
air.

What ailed the sea that it fled? What ailed the mountains,
the romping lambs
Bought with blood? Tremble, earth, before the Lord of the
Crow and the Dove
Who turned flint into fountain, created the fruit of the vine
devoured by the

Fox who bit the dog that worried the cat that killed the rat
that ate up Jack
Who built the house: Yisgaddal v'yiskaddash sh'meh rabbo
— miracle of seed,
Mystery of rain, the ripening sun and the failing flesh,
courses of stars,

Stress from Sinai:

> Let (roared God)

>> Great big Babylon
>> Be eaten up by Persia
>> Be eaten up by Greece
>> Be eaten up by Rome
>> Be eaten up by Ottoman
>> Be eaten up by Edom
>> Be eaten by Australia
>> Where Jack's house shook.

> Be (said Jack's Dad)

>> Submissive to an elder
>> Courteous to the young
>> Receive all men with
>> Cheerfulness and
>> Hold your tongue.

Strangers, remember Jack who did as he was told.

*   *   *

To the goddess the blood of all creatures is due for she gave it,
Temple and slaughterhouse, maker of curses like
worm-eaten peas:

As the thunder vanishes, so shall the woman drive them
away
As wax melts before flame, so let the ungodly perish before
her:

She is mother of thunder, mother of trees, mother of lakes,
Secret springs, gate to the underworld, vessel of darkness,

Bearer, transformer, dark nourisher, shelterer, container of
Living and dead, coffin of Osiris, dark-egg devourer
engenderer,

66

Nurturer, nurse of the world, many-armed goddess girdled
by cobras,
Flame-spewer, tiger-tongued queen of the dead and the
violent dancers.

Mother of songs, dancer of granite, giver of stone —
Let his wife speak:

"Honour thy father and thy mother"
So have I done and done and done — no marriage shall ever

Consume the black maidenhead — my parents are heaven
Bound. I shall rejoin them;

Bodies of men shall rejoin severed souls
At the ultimate blast of invisible grace.

Below, I burn,
Naomi of the long brown hair, skull in a Juliet cap.

Do the dead rot? Then rot as I rot as they rot.
"Honour thy Father" sing Armistice bells, *espressivo*.

The stumbling fingers are groping
To pitch of perfection.

I am that pitch
I am that perfection.

Papa's a civilian again, mother is coiled in a corset,
Dispenses perfection with:

Castor oil
Tapestry
Tablecloths (white)
Rectal thermometers
Czerny and prunes
Sonatinas of Hummel

The white meat of chicken
The white meat of fish
The maids and the lost silver.

Lord, I am good for nothing, shall never know want.

Blinded, I burn, am led not into temptation.

The home is the centre of power.
                    There I reign
Childless. Three daughters, all whores, all —

Should be devoured by the fires of Gehenna
Should be dissolved in the womb that bore them
Should wander the wastelands forever.

Instead, they dance.

Whole towns condemn me. Flames from the roofs
Form my father's fiery image. He waves, laughs,

Cools his head among stars, leaves me shorn,
Without sons, unsanctified, biting on

Bread of affliction. Naked, I burn,
Orphaned again in a war.

The world is a different oyster:
Mine.

His defection will not be forgotten.

* * *

Blessed be He whose law speaks of the three different
characters of children whom
we are to instruct on this occasion:

What says the wicked one?

"What do you all mean by this?"
This thou shalt ask not, and thou hast transgressed, using
you and excluding thyself.

Thou shalt not exclude thyself from:

The collective body of the family
The collective body of the race
The collective body of the nation

Therefore repeat after me:

"This is done because of what the Eternal did
For me when I came forth from Egypt."

The wicked wants always the last word (for all the good
it does): "Had I been there, I would still not be worth

My redemption." Nothing more may be eaten, a beating will
Take place in the laundry. Naked.

"Honour thy father and thy mother"

What says the wise one?

"The testimonies, statutes, the judgments delivered by God I
accept."

Nonetheless, though thou are wise,
After the paschal offering there shall be no dessert.

"Honour thy father and thy mother"

What says the simple one?

Asks merely: "What is this?"

Is told: "With might of hand

Did our God bring us forth out of Egypt
From the mansion of bondage."

Any more questions? Ask away and be damned.

"Honour thy father and thy mother"

* * *

Yisborach, v'yistabach, v'yispoar, v'yisroman, v'yisnaseh,
v'yishaddor,
v'yisalleh, v'yishallol, sh'meh d'kudsho, b'rich hu

Praise death who is our God
Live for death who is our God
Die for death who is our God
Blessed be your failure which is our God

Oseh sholom bim'romov, hu yaaseh sholom, olenu v'al kol
yisroel, v'imru Omen.

* * *

And he who was never born and cannot inquire shall say:

There is a time to speak
and a time to be silent
There is a time to forgive
and a time in which to be
Forgiven.
After forgiveness,

Silence.

Cleft

One night she headless gave away the
old world, dreamed anew. Men tall and
small and pretty thin slid in
and out of her like
maddened trombones, blasting
her scales. The emptied armour
lay wherein she trusted, tranced,

The hollow vizor's chamber breathed
its last guffaw before
matters got really serious
even at a pinch you might say out of
hand at which nice point the
severed head, wide-eyed with loss
danced towards her orchestrated

Trunk, ready (as ever) with a few
home academic truths: "Deluded and
unconscious woman! Enact your matey
operations, revisit life, visit the
dead, forage the skull, the skin
the skin," it moaned, "but shot you
are of my sublimity." The groaning

trombones strained in *Liebestod* and,
thickening on her tongue, the dream
did in the dawn.

Dreams

Sleeping badly, he'd wake in a rage
to recover the loss. Loss of what?
He could never be sure. At his age
(hardly love but a spasm perhaps?)

A tight squeeze of the heart — nothing more
he'd assure himself, breathing alone in the
darkness. Yet why did he look to the door
as if something had come and was gone?

Mysterious injury, ill and yet never quite
ill enough, it would seem (for a time)
as if she'd never been. By the light
of a day he'd see a girl walking away

In the rain — a casual profile, the turn
of a wrist, the drop of a head. She
didn't exist, had never. He'd learn
to forget, to begin to forget

He would sleep again. Obscurely and peacefully dead
to the world, breathing easy. Yet suddenly dreaming,
awake to himself in the dark of the bed, somewhere
in an endless passage started to howl.

The Artist

(after Isaac Bashevis Singer)

She spoke the word "artist"
as seriously as a pious Jew
names God. Naive?

You bet, and tall
with it — a brown-eyed
40'ish female of a kind

they don't make nowadays.
Not, I believe, a barbarian
but almost, I was after

a couple of stories: "I
guess you'd call me one,"
I muttered, taking notes.

She took all poetry seriously
which goes to show she
wasn't on the uptake. I

set myself to shock her,
a full bottle on brothels
and the confession of sins.

I had material for years to
serve her with, defamed all
poets from old Shelley on

and told her I was fucking
five (women, that is) at the
same time, the words as near

the gutter as I could. To
comfort me for being so misguided
she delivered books and cake

and finally herself: "You
are so gifted, so deluded
why sink you so in darkness?"

(such flowery phrases came to
her quite naturally), and I a
chronic liar laughed, told

truths however brutal, watched
her eyes take fire from
life's injustice to the

gifted of this world. And
still alive, she'd answer
as if I were hardly there at all:

"You are an artist.
God will forgive you
for your talent."

Identity

"Our greatest joys to mark an outline truly
And know the piece of earth on which we stand."
So you may say, and I in part accept the newly
Taken exploration of a whispering land,

But voices in the country of the mind
Tame the crueller aspect of my days.
Irresolute as fine weather, I am blind
With memories. Nature was never friendly, her ways

Severed me and serious poets should never be severed,
Should lovers be, namers of colours, shapes, plants.
Not urban neurotics from frustrate armchairs levered
To stare through glass at bird-forsaken haunts.

Nature poets are rarely as tranquil or composed
As they sound. Wordsworth fussed around, man
Speaking to God, not men — delight imposed
On distraction. John Clare ate weeds. Cowper ran

Mad from the world's disease. Their city hell
My heaven, their order my darkness. "One vast mill"
Can compass rival landscapes. So I'll sell
The poet's soul for memory's Eden, whirl

The glass above the ravenous soil split
Wide in veined caverns, shaped by affliction.
Seeded in flame, hatched to withstand, I'll pit
Double-tongued desert winds against my conviction.

After Such Knowledge

Disaster around. She has worked hard
at it. Sneer, sniff, cavil, carp

Sunder the muddy dignities but
dignities despite. Lovers, husbands,

Children, friends alive, dead or
halfway dead steam off.

Half cracked with hope she
wheels on the ocean bed below

Their wake, dull bell tongueless
from a cold tower, snagged in weeds.

In what sweet silence rests the bell unless,
bearing a royal pardon, little ships return?

Reckoning

Whom have We next? (His syntax is
perfect). This one is due for what
there is called joy.
                              I alone know
the span of her schooling.
Who else needs to know?
None but I, the Omnipotent.
Under my hat will I keep it
(vernacular master).
                              Her sullen
green fires will I spring
unburden her airs
allow time to pass
and in My pain's darkness
trample her glass.

Three Songs of Love & Hate

1 *The Stone Dolphin*

I have prayed for the end of his breath
(and mine)
to what end?

Anger's words have been hugged
and released.
The language of tyranny had to be
learnt if anything were to be said.

What has been said has been said
is still said after the panting
mouth has been clamped by despair.
But led by the devils
do angels leave too?

True grief is tongueless when the dumb
define love's death.
In a fiercely fathered and unmothered world
words are wrung from the rack.

Bury love's face
Bury love's bones
Bury love's tongue
in a place where the cataract groans,
where water is wedded to stones.

My dolphin, you'll leap in the sun,
Caught sweet, without hate,
Without grief in perpetual summer.
I sang you through gentler seas
than you knew, nor will know never.
Time full and perfect made heaven to
laugh in its mercy, made flower the apple,
showered me with innocent petals,
shook birds and fish in the lightning
tides where wind and water merge, melt,
melt and forever melt.

Drowned in the boon of his breath
I gave thanks for his dolphin pride,
for the creatures of water and air
keeping our pace.
Even the airs of the oncoming night
couldn't chill our far fathoming.

Warned, yet unwarned, beguiled by far
kinder griefs, swimming alone and
drowning, I embraced in one
shining sun track a dolphin of stone.

2   *Jack Frost*

To sit upon her belly warm
Jack Frost has come.
His cold sweet weight
Does not alarm the night
Or shake belief.

Too cold to ache
She parts her leaves
And welcomes thrust of snow
And stretches fingers past all pain
To stroke the teasing foe.

The cold creeps on
The buds unfold and burn
Her into night. Traversed
She lies and powerless to
Thaw the subtle guest.

3 Tiger Heart

The tiger heart (if heart it is)
Kneels down within its cage
It laps the famished air
It asks for nothing more.

Orpheus sings alone to master
Nature, stills its rage.
The smallest bird abashed, is
Warmed, the fish fly water,
Spring to him, the wind and sea
Are mute. The trees and stones
March steadily, the river flowing
Upward to the dulcet chant
Springs golden shrimp, anemone.
The lamb and wolf are teased
by hope, they look upon the face
of love appeased, but all's not sure —

The tiger stoops within its cage
And keeps its starving course along.
It will not hear the song.

Lamb

The people press.
They gaze and call it "star".
To me it's time for home.
The winking silver points mean
"Stars" — there are so many.
They mean
My master's loving clasp
My mother's tit
And sleep. Then all is black
Till morning.

This is its mother too.
A straw hangs on her lip
And all the folk are sighing for
The little creature as they
Sighed when I dropped bloody
From my mother's hole.
I didn't know then why
They sighed but am beginning.
Cold winds and snows,
The black of night,
Force all of us to kneel.

Ark Voices

i Mrs Noah Speaks

Lord, the cleaning's nothing.
What's a pen or two?
Even if the tapir's urine
Takes the paint clean off
There's nothing easier.

But sir, the care!

I used to dream perpetually
About a boat I had to push
(yes, *push*) through a stony town
without water
There was no river and no sea and yet
I pushed a boat against a tide.
It wouldn't float although I pulled and
hauled, my flesh eddying,
drifting with the strain of it.
Is *this* a dream?
Fibre my blood, sir.

The speckled pigeon and the tawny owl
swoop by
                    They coax me to the edge.

To save to save merely — no matter
what or whom — to save.

Sweep and push of waves against the sides.
Our raft is delicate and our fire
turns wood to ashes.

He takes it well
and Shem and Ham do help — you can't expect
too much of anyone can you and
Japhet's still a kid. Their wives are
young and tremble in the rain
their wits astray.
As soon as we're born
we're all astray — at least
you seem to think it's so or else
why this?

I know you promised us a landing but
what a price!
We're dashed from side to side
we strike through spray
the foam blinds Noah till he
cannot steer.
Even the mightiest creature cowers in his
stall panting, snorting in the welter,
bursting prayers upon your path
of righteousness.

Comfort enough I'm not.
To feed and clothe, to bind a scratch I can.

We once moved quiet in our lives
Looked steadily ahead. When I was small
there were no roads across the mountains
no boats or bridges over water.
We farmed, live simple, circumscribed.
Our birds and beasts delivered their young
in peace. The trees grew tall and now and
then I pocketed a speckled egg, could climb
and peer into the nests of starlings.
Height and blossom.

Then we lived neighbourly with our birds.
Creation, your handiwork, was one.
No good and bad — just men and women.
But with your sages came the rub.

                We tripped
over our charity. Duty-fettered, love
tumbled like a lightning-stricken tower.

Noah is incorruptible and good, a large
sweet soul.
Sir, I have tried to be!
But does the frog whose home was in a well
assail an ocean?
How does the summer gnat approach the ice?
The flood in which you throne us is to the
universe a puddle in a marsh.

                  Of all the myriad
creatures you have made, man is but one, the
merest tip of hair upon a stallion's rump.

Noah looks into space.
He sees the small as small
The great as great.
He sees, goes fearless at the sight.
I see the small as too little
the great as too much.
Does this diminish me?

He looks back to the past
grieves not over what is distant.
I mourn the wrack, the rock under the
blue sea, our old wound, the
dismantling storm and cannot
thank you.

            Helpless with what I am
what can I do? This pitted flesh and
madness in my heart, rage at my fear
of you. Am I thus harmless?

Strangers in this ark, this one small 'Yes'
afloat on a vast "No", your watery negative.

Noah stares impassive through the foam.
I trust in him although our woe, the
trap of my young body, cracked his trust
in me.
            I bend but do not break under your
chilling stars.

Even the wolves, the tigers must be fed
in these deep-laden waters. Else we are
all drowned bones.
                        Intercede with him
for me, speechless and unspoken to, the
comic keeper of his house.
My sons are fraught with wives, have
waded into deep waters.
A full ship and homeward bound — Yes,
I'm just about to lance the horse's leg.
A large sweet soul and incorruptible
I said. Or have I seen the great as
too much yet again?
                        The speckled pigeon
and the tawny owl have drawn me to the edge.
The drowned folk call to me:
Deliver us from harm!

Deliver, sir, deliver them
and all of us...

ii *Lemur*

This powerful tail this tiny brain
Would make of man an ass:

Because of such as me the earth is riven.
Yet I suit your plan and am

Forgiven for it. Lord, you
Surge me clear of pain:

Nor past nor future, duty nor
Regret are mine.

Today today today only
Today I swing upon my ring —

Tailed rung from sleep to sleep to
Hunger Play Sleep to

Leap through blackest night.
A state of grace.

Laved in eternal rhythms
My ailing howls kill time:

We eat and die.

Your eye burns a dark
Angelic arc into my frightened fur.

The rəin will wash it clean
Away — before me the flood —

Io Lemuria! Wandering spirit of the dead
Voracious once a year revisit
Those I loved who feed me quick,
Thud wide the door, and shaking pray:

"Manes exite Paterni!"
Leave! Ghosts of our fathers!

Grafted with their pain I go
Only to return

Sir, I fear my part in this haunting

iii Bat

Born bat-blind
wawled naked
into flight,
parent-pocketed.

     I swerve
from light, see through
my crazy stiffening ears.

Hang-glider of your flood
Sir, I skim
             and
                  whirl
                        dark water.

        Struts extended,
prop thin skin against your
withering blast.

Whirring within the ark,
claws lurch to clutch at
crevice memories, the hollows
of a feeding dusk.

Come night, and Noah ducks my
fine fur, accurate flap, my
craven pointed face.

My nostrils trail spirals of
shrill screams.

I'm more afraid
did they but know what you
have always known:

by day I hang
like one condemned
to die

iv Mouse

Though you attend my body, Sir
my high thin cry,
can you bear me in mind?

Before your rim I bob I
whisk and skitter, drill
my mate — O cordial seed-shower!

Humbly born I take your father-
nature on me, eat my young. To
rise again unscathed though

Far fallen. The merest crack in
your creation makes me visible:
small hole in a ripe corn basket.

Docile I fit beneath mine enemy's
foot, sole privacy of death.
Your seas add nothing to my daily

Fear. You prepare me coriander
carraway, stout barley, lentils,
poppy in presence of my foes,

restrain the green-eyed devil
monstering me, forestall the
leaning elephant, remind the

hamster weasel stoat rat that

Ashore and in one room
no cockroach can survive
a loose and starving mouse

v Mink

In so meek a slink
lies ambush.
　　My soft tail
disarms.

Sir, my dreams are violent
even as your waters crash
great trees to earth
like matchsticks.

　　Beast that I am
I frolic: why dream beyond this
life so succulent?

My fires leap to the stream's
flow and in a wood I know
whatever moves:
　　spring
　　　　scuttle
　　　　　　scrabble
　　　　　　　　claw

fury of frisk and gore
and the long strong smell
of a death.

　　Close to water merge with
mallard frog heron spiny lobster.
　　Whatever moves
is still thereafter.

Immoderate scabrous fisher-king, should I
complain my soul's bitterness? Instead I
eavesdrop on the river's descant
note the soft mottled trout bellies
luminous transparencies of water life.

I trap,
kill as those made in your image trap me
to wear and warm.

Such silence under fragile leaves
before the spring.

Taken alive my face is known
to wear the devil's cast:

beautiful moon-drinker
sun-swallower

vi Wolf-Song

Cold blows the wind in the forest,
And quietly drops the snow,
I never had but one lover,
And her grave lies here below
And her grave lies here below.

I'll sing of her death in the forest,
The loveliest of them all,
I'll howl and run in the quiet snow
Till they answer to my call
Till they answer to my call.

They can beat their drum in the thorny brake
They can blow their horn in the town,
My cry shall wake the very dead,
And I shall run them down
And I shall run them down.

Saddled and bridled and booted,
Came three hunters to the vale,
They caroused with the townsfolk merry.
And were told a painful tale
And were told a painful tale.

"There are wolves in our windy forest
There are wolves in our snow-bound plain,
Our sheep and our children are taken
And will ne'er come back again
And will ne'er come back again.

When the moon shines white in the forest,
You can hear them moan and cry,
They hunt by scent in our peaceful vale
And our children all will die
And our children all will die."

Then up rose the gallant hunters,
They took out gun and knife
They swore they would rid the snow-bound vale
Of the wolves who halted life
Of the wolves who halted life.

They came on horseback at midnight,
They came with knife and gun,
My love and I did howl and cry
And their nimble hounds did run
And their nimble hounds did run.

They came to a break in the forest,
They heard our guiltless cry,
The foremost of the company
Took aim against the sky
Took aim against the sky.

The hounds ran swiftly through the wood
My tender love to take,
And from the very hills and dales
An echo shrill did shake
An echo shrill did shake.

And now there came the panting hounds
And now there came the gun
The foremost levelled it at my love
As helpless we did run
As helpless we did run.

O he has killed my one true love!
O he has killed my dear!
Her blood is springing on the snow,
And I am stiff with fear
And I am stiff with fear.

Whose blood is this in the forest?
What moon shines clear in the sky?

Though I have to wait out seven years
The hunters will surely die
The hunters will surely die.

I've ravaged their sheep by night
I've slaughtered their children by day
O sweet shall I sing to see their blood
Which for that death shall pay
Which for that death shall pay.

The seventh year is upon me
Seven years from her final breath,
I'll howl and run in the silent snow
And lure them to their death
And lure them to their death.

I'll sing of her end in the forest,
The loveliest of them all,
I'll howl and run in the bloody snow
Till they answer to my call
Till they answer to my call.

You can rest, my love, in our forest,
You can sleep in our thorny brake,
For the hunters three today will die
And I their life shall take
And I their life shall take.

O when shall we meet, my dear one?
O when shall we meet again?
When the leaves are fallen from the bough
And the green and the spring are come
And the green and the spring are come.

vii Tiger

Lord, you know as well as I
who made this fearful symmetry
and why

Truth needs no sign.

Your ark's eaves fret my stride
my pad sinks heavy on this narrow spot
its cubits warp my stalk
hunched for your
sore slaughter.

Beating through unknown currents
veiled cataracts of foam
drench the high hills where
once I preyed.

    Was I not your pride
when first I parted paleolithic fronds to
roll my mate, renew our undefiled
bone and flesh?

Fair as the moon
clear as the sun
terrible as an army with gold-brown banners
on me you set your heart's seal:
son of morning.

Your love was stronger than death.
Your new moons were my delight.
You worshipped the work of your hands.
Howl, gate! Cry, city!
Whelms me the trap of your vast wing.

I'd lief lick up the swollen waters
of your wrath than,
competent to kill, be
smothered in safety:

who would so starved survive?

viii Hipposonnets

He

Weary with toil, my ugly head is large,
My baggy muzzle ponders to the earth,
Against you, sir, I lay my plaintive charge:
That you have sanctioned such misshapen birth
As mine. You call me your creation fair,
Bulbous and rude, I dive into your flood,
Warty and naked, rough beyond repair,
I thirst for beauty. My sluggish substance would
Offend the very bottom of the lake.
I mince upon my well-developed toes.
Snorting violent columns, rise to take
The air with swift extremity. My nose
Seeks out my love timid and perfect, but find
Only my grief, and all my joy behind.

She

Yawning I lingered, drowsy took my ways
Along the high banks, dreaming of my desire:
A single offspring, tenant of my days
To guard and nurture. Shaped in disabling fire
I laboured the monthly courses of the moon,
Met with the loose dull substance of my kind
And suddenly the inventive act was done.
Our wrinkled baby pads along behind
Our ponderous puzzled flesh. He nuzzles warm
Against me. The small bright interim of our love
Blunts my tusks to lift him clear of harm,
Your perfect creation. Sir, if I could prove
The fitness of my longings, would it serve
To know, just for the record, that once I loved?

ix Giraffe

Front legs spraddled wide
     neck arched
       delicate
      down
      I
     sip O sir
    your rough waters

Within the ark I stifle
paceless, acute spectator,
mustard-and-orange brawn
sky-bather

Why not excess undo and
dock me?
down to size expose me to
feel what others feel, see
what others see.

Taller, more abject I
strip acacia's highest leaves
towards which others strain
fail
fall
short and I long
witness enemies and warn
with soft blunt horn.

To whose advantage?
I'd rather mingle vision
with the ant than, so
removed, command the
lion and the leopard
in my sight.

whirr

I jitter whinnying
kick   bite   bolt
at shadows:
                    dappled
forelimb and hindlimb
rock over yellow plains in
blue-hoofed funk. Fly-wisk tail
corkscrews behind: kind winds
favour clownish miles.

Motionless mottle
I blend: am
sun-patches
leaf-clusters
everything
nothing

x *Whale Psalm*

I steer the chastened furrows
with my tail
coil filamented upwards   lift   thrash
down to
crash the
heaving waste
behind.

My captors close
upon me, sir, I call —

          Thew and sinew
peak and plunge: then softly softly
stealthy roll and glide, recoil to
coil again

            lift in subtle curvature
plunge downward:
my ponderous flukes subdue
the darkening flood.

           O sir, you thus
prepared me, thus I churned your path
chanted your praise: my being
spoke your wonder.

         Unmoored from innocence
from your sight cast, today I range
hell's belly.

Earth's nets tighten:
men forsake their mercy, shroud me dumb
who have so loved the habitation of
your waters.

Rein me from darkness now as once
you ransomed Nineveh lest
fishers mourn, nets languish
on the blackening sea.

xi Elephant

I bulge in my bindings, dream-wrinkled,
dreaming of long slow rivers:
I rend with my pent-up proboscis
your buffeting seas.

                      Pendulous delicate
hybrid of handnostrilnerve; glorious
once could raise rocks, split trunks
pull feathers from air, pluck
nestling from nest.

                  Then rest,
silted in shadow.

Once could paw up jungles in thunder
and trumpets: with one foot wrench
kingdoms asunder, intercept missions
of stars:

war-fossil
power-shard
hack hierophant
temple dancer

now plod mud-slumberous
sluiced in this world's waters
dreaming of long slow rivers
and you, sir

        the source
        the source
        the source

The Poet Gives a Reading

He told them all about himself
and what his parents did to him
and how though lazy
he once showed a slight
but quite exceptional
gift for tinkering
with radios.

How his parents also showed
exceptional patience.
Plenty of expense and trouble
sent him east to study
radio and still more
radio but he couldn't hear
the words
couldn't follow
even the simplest
instruction.

Efforts had been made
Yes,
efforts had been made
to make him normal
O so normal.

He seemed so quick-witted
sane and even
sometimes sensible,
with reasonably earnest
intentions he told them
all about what it was like
to be married to his
wife, what it was like
to be
a father.

He read his favourite
poem about love and walked
up and down up and
down
Then
read another poem not
about his wife but
also about love
or so he said,
and reading walked
up and down
up and down, his thumb
stuck sharp in a brass-
studded belt, buckle winking
as a tow-haired student
asked were poets
real and meaningful
people.

O yes, he said
real enough as
real goes.
A regular western child
I was —
my mother needled my
father cold, my father
drank his pay away and I
stayed young in my
mind as your regular
children do
he said walking up and
down, up and down
his thumb grown
restless in his belt
like the thumbs of
regular children will
when the dragon-shaped
cloud hovers over the hill

and the day turns up
to his wakening look.

A seaman's son with
eyes of blue who walked
up and down like a
stealthy screw
and said about read
about more about love
than your regular
children
do
pinning messages on the
jotting-pad of his mind
to a girl in
white with a dark Indian face
who left after the
second last poem
with a barely
concealed
yawn

The Poet Puts It Away

Keeping his beard on, he moved
into hand-stitched shoes
7-league suits: the buckle's
wink was dim.

Losing altitude he
entered the "diviner heaven of prose":
getting closer to himself.
Out of gear
and often in the wrong key,
had haemorrhoids, was ethically in a
mess and, for the umpteenth time, his
daemonic was slipping.

Scholarly research can
excavate the problem from St Paul
till 1980: called psychohistory,
some things are better left alone.

More subjectively
and not sober, he indicted equally
Dr Heinrich Hoffman (circa 1840) and
his mother (definitely 1907 although
she preferred 1915) for cutting him off
in all directions:

"The door flew open, in he ran,
The great, long, red-legg'd scissorman
Oh! children see! the tailor's come
And caught our little Suck-a-Thumb"

A close shave either way.
Ever alert for women booze and chocolate
he committed 354 fornications (at least

half were under-age) off his own bat
though he called it "getting laid":

"Mama had scarcely turn'd her back,
The thumb was in, Alack! Alack!"

Countless airy lies
laid out like glowing rugs for his
imaginative inspection; constant coveting
of his neighbour's ass (he moved house
often); the theft of three books:

the Gideon Bible from the
Port Hedland Motor Hotel
(the word of God ought to
be free and the Gideons
whoever they are want you
to steal it so they can put
another in its place for
another lying Priapus to
simmer down with after
multiple campus fucks);
Aristotle's *Nichomachean Ethics*
(which he assumed nobody would
ever read and he never got
around to it either); and
Henry Miller's *Cosmological Eye*
(which ought to have proved
orgasmic but turned out to be
vaguely mystic and
put him to sleep. Quickly).

Two cats and a dog met their end by
his motor vehicle, a thousand
winged insects by his hand:

"Here is cruel Frederick, see!
A horrid wicked boy was he"

His father was anything but honoured
his mother positively dishonoured,
hacked up, hidden and easily discovered:

"Let me see if Frederick can
Be a little gentleman"

Took God's name in vain daily
put himself inexorably into every
poem without even a decorous
pretence of self-distrust for which
he received high praise.

Slandered the
Sicilian next door, put away
5000 litres of whisky in
10 years, made his wives
altars of stone and
sacrificed them to
punk rock:

and no (with a sideways look)
today he wasn't friendly either.

Erect in the middle of
thunderings and lightnings
he struck:
more poems in him
than he'd hoped for but
more than he wished.

They
had a way of telling
the truth and believing
himself alone in the
storm he heard
none of it.

The Poet Asks Forgiveness

Dead to the world I have failed you
Forgive me, traveller.

Thirsty, I was no fountain
Hungry, I was not bread
Tired, I was no pillow

Forgive my unwritten poems:
the many I have frozen with irony
the many I have trampled with anger
the many I have rejected in self-defence
the many I have ignored in fear

unaware, blind or fearful
I ignored them.
They clamoured everywhere
those unwritten poems.
They sought me out day and night
and I turned them away.

Forgive me the colours
they might have worn
Forgive me their eclipsed faces
They dared not venture from
the unwritten lines.

Under each inert hour of my silence
died a poem, unheeded

Ask Me

I

China Poems 1988

I *Roosters and Earthworms*

It's the year of the Dragon.
Omens for the journey aren't encouraging.
No language and I'm booked
on China Airlines. In Hong Kong I dream
that I am born without a tongue
and wake up screaming…

I'm studying the twelve animal signs.
Or did the Revolution do away with them?
Too frivolous maybe? The Irish in me
thinks there may be something in it
all the same. Keep reading —

Are you a sentimental but crafty Rat?
A dutiful Ox?
A smashing but unpredictable Tiger?
I am a Rooster.
Honest, frank, obliging, difficult
to live with.
Spot on, so far. What's this?
Vain? Despotic? Prickly about criticism?
Perhaps there's nothing in it
after all.

Tradition has it that I'd find
an earthworm in the desert.

My best roles are military hero or clown.
Not much to choose between them but
I'll settle for the latter, never liked
the army much (the Irish rises up again),
My worst is spy — I'm too conspicuous.

Roosters don't mean to hurt your feelings.
They simply like to let you know
your food's inedible, your hygiene's foul,
your creature comforts nil, you're vain,
despotic, prickly about criticism.

Rooster celebrities include:
Catherine the Great, Colette, Copernicus
and Kierkegaard (the company's not improving),
Marie de Medici, Strindberg, Queen Victoria
and, wouldn't you know, Wagner.

I'd better watch myself.
Plenty of other roosters on the farm.
Earthworms never grew on trees.
This is where it all began.

II Out of this World

I'm in Beijing.
When I was young it was Peking.
Fans and silk and lacquered screens,
sages playing chess in elegant pavilions
on the Flowery Mountain...

It's minus 4.
The heating system thumped all night,
the cistern trickled.
At school we called it Chinese Torture,
gave each other Chinese Burns.
China was a name to conjure with
when we were young, light-years away,
out of this world.

It's 5.30 a.m. and I've been downstairs twice.
Nobody there.

Down in a vast reading room for students
I saw two dogeared journals, *China Reconstructs*,
in a bookcase with glass doors.
Not a book in sight.
Someone left a Chinese newspaper.
I can't read a word. Who am I here?

The water taps are dry.
The colours in my room bring back
Australian holidays, dead brown grainless
pub wardrobes, kitchen-green walls,
dun green felt carpeting.
Under the bed with its embroidered pillowslip
lie two used plastic scuffs. They're also green.
There's a tall red anodised thermos
flanked by two sachets of coarse tea-leaves,
rough as bonsai'd mallee roots. Two mugs with lids.
Something square stands sheathed in black.

Velvet and sinister, it's in a corner.
I lift a flap. A TV set, the antenna's
a Chinese character inside a hoop of steel.
Two diabolic little horns point upward.
Many knobs, a cord, no powerpoint.
I lift the phone.
It buzzes like a thousand swarming bees.
I put it down.

Don't look out the window yet.
Try to deal with what's inside.

At 6 the water starts.
My bath looks like the Red River.
I slumber in the river, part of me
awake on CA Flight 309, marking
before the symptom "if any now"
Fever   Rash   Cough
Bleeding   Psychosis   Leprosy
Aids
I've got them all.

The river's still,
becalmed above red sediment.

Below the window on a concrete path
a man in black stands motionless.
Black gloves, black coat, a cap.
Is he really standing there
below my bathroom window?
I look hard again holding my breath.
He's there all right.

He's all alone.
The dawn is rising red before him.
He doesn't know or care
that there's a frightened watcher
following his stillness like a dream.

But he's turning slowly now   slowly
like a dream he turns and folds his hands
as if in slowest prayer
first one side and then slowly
to the other, light-years away
and out of this world.

He isn't young.

III Over the Wall

Today we go to the Wall.
The sun shines, the bus is small.

We loose Australians pile obediently in.
We laugh moderately.
One of us is making a joke.
We can't go overboard here.

Later we'll go over the top
of the Wall. When we get out.

Our two guardians sit up straight
in Mao jackets up the front,
between them a neat pile of paper bags.
Our playlunch.

We're diplomatic and attentive.
I hardly recognise us.

Far down the back sit students.
They are quiet and gentle.
They don't go overboard either.
They may not get out
until the visitors have left.

The sun shines on.
We climb the Wall.
The magic mountains better all our dreams,
their peaks razored against
an endless sky.

Clearly their painters invented nothing.
Looked and recorded
looked and recorded the changeless
whetstoned cones with maybe a man
somewhere down in a corner,
very small and very wise.

We climb and look again.
The eye oscilloscopes along and back
along and back...

A student carrying my bag is watching me.
She smiles. "You like it here?"
How can I tell her that
I'm neither happy nor unhappy?

How can I tell her that I've seen
a man at the foot of these ageless peaks
a man who has turned away,
a man who is very small and very wise?

She might think I was seeing things.

IV Passing

Dreams are the suicides of the well-behaved.

Do the Chinese have great and wonderful powers
of forgetfulness?
Or do they dream like anybody else?

I met a man living in the same building
as the man who killed his father.

He refused to take the lift
in case he met this man.

He walks up six flights of stairs twice a day.
The lift passes up and down slowly
and he watches the iron cage pass.

I dream a poor boy's dream of China,
the story of silence.
The men who pass his father's grave each day,
and walking, raise their caps slowly
without speaking.

Tiananmen Square
June 4, 1989

Karl Marx, take your time,
looming over Highgate on your plinth.
Snow's falling on your beard,
exiled, huge, hairy, genderless.
Terminally angry, piss-poor,
stuffed on utopias and cold,
cold as iron.

I'm thinking of your loving wife,
your desperate children and your grandchild
dead behind the barred enclosure of your brain.
Men's ideas the product, not the cause
of history, you said?

The snow has killed the lilacs.
Whose idea?
The air is frozen with theory.

What can the man be doing all day
in that cold place?
What can he be writing?
What can he be reading?
What big eyes you have, mama!
Next year, child, we will eat.

I'm thinking of my middle-class German grandmother
soft as a pigeon, who wept
when Chamberlain declared a war.
Why are you crying, grandma?
It's only the big bad wolf, my dear.
It's only a story.

There's no end to it.
The wolves have come again.
What shall I tell my grandchildren?

No end to the requiems, the burning trains,
the guns, the shouting in the streets,
the outraged stars, the anguished face
of terror under ragged headbands
soaked in death's calligraphy.

Don't turn your back, I'll say.
Look hard.
Move into that frozen swarming screen.
How far can you run with a bullet in your brain?

And forgive, if you can, the safety of a poem
sharpened on a grieving night.

A story has to start somewhere.

The Temple, Somnapura

*Choose for your Stone him through whom
kings are honoured in their crowns,
and through whom physicians heal their
sick, for he is near to the fire.*

        Rosarium philosophorum (1550)

I Ganesh

Footfall
smooth   cool
soothing the sole
arched and released
soundless in
underworld spaces

tread inward
down and
down   slow
slow
lightening the arch
press   swaying on
smoothness on
oiled pilgrimed
soles softened
to yearning
stone
down

Footfall
released arch
loosed to the
edge
the edge

and down
inward
inward —

Faith is the sound
of a man breathing
alone in darkness
emptied

Faith is his patience
tenure on foot-fastened
stone
prayer to an
absence

To learn the Emptiness of the bare mind
Without knowledge . . .

Is truth so smooth
so bald
so stark
so dumb as temple stone?

A light shaft strikes the stone,
mints spry slumped corpulent Ganesh,
elephant-crowned runt
of jealous Siva,
the enormous first parent —

Grant, O Lord, we beseech Thee
won't do here —

Affliction fathers gods and men,
our first shame equal.

Ganesh learns his ponderous bulk
upon the open world, his trunk
ripples with laughter.

Pad slow   slow
moulding the foot
to the swell and the fall
the cool stone
breathing —

Echoes swirl the ancient ceiling
voices   voices
cries in little flames lick
sacred texts in smoke
half-caught forms
bells   incense
    dung

Light the tall bronze lamps.
Feed them oil.
Twist the wicks to flicker
over blue-black hair —

Siva's eye beheads his son
and there he sits, docked,
bowed in elephantine sorrow.

Even gods may be ambiguous,
hate their wives,
their children.

His hands fold slyly in prayer,
lips part like shells
to whispering waves of stone —

Women kneel in pious shadows
tracing sinuous whorls of coloured flour,
wisped by incense.
Blue-black oiled hair, white gleaming
cluster upon cluster climb,
trembling jasmine, nightshade, marigolds
garlands of orange   green   gold —

Astride a bandicoot
lord Ganesh laughs.
A short fat marvellous child
bulbous bright, four arms
blistered with bees
three eyes behind his
rippling trunk —

Slumbering in stone
he leans upon the whispers of the dark,
night's nursery.
His fine molested grace remembers
promises of love
towards his difference:

Indra's goad
Padmavati's lotus
coloured inks from Sarasvati
a tiger skin from father Siva
a sacrificial thread from
roaring Brihaspati.
And from the goddess Earth, a rat
to draw his stunting chariot.

Becalmed in stone
his lotus face smiles down
amused and absent —

Retreating from the light
of his now-fathering force,
our human shadows print us small
like crippled children.

II Vishnu

No precepts here
but slow unravellings —

   Vish
      nu
  Kri
     shn
avish
   nu
    Krish
    na
       a a a a

pitched against the One
the One forever changeless God
who swaddles mutinous children's hands
and stops their mouth —

The body and the soul know how to play
In that dark world where gods have lost their way.

Light air and silence kiss
the lazy lotus lip.
Vishnu, rapt in fleshless sleep
under his curly crown,
once tumultuous

The sun, a scorching nectarine
rolls aside the misty scarves
wreathing the violet blur of
distant hills. Green hosts of parakeets
all shriek and blaze and dazzle
divine the coming of the god. Morning quicke.
mounts. All moves and sways suspended.

The body and the soul know how to play
In that dark world where gods have lost their way.
             — Theodore Roethke, "The Partner"

Tilting crows cut ever-widening circles high
above the creaking sway of carts
a steady bullock chomp of straw.
Well-wheels grinding grinding grinding
tiny matchstick forms dot out
the hazy wakening fields,
the long slow hum of breathless morning.

Pensive wives of cowherds toss
on tousled beds.
Come, lord Krishna, hear their song:

"My pillow won't tell me
Where he has gone,
The soft-footed one
Who passed by, alone.

Who took my heart whole,
With a tilt of his eye,
And with it, my soul,
And it like to die."

Our lord with lotus eyes
has raised a mountain.
Dark as storm his blue-black wings
lift all of us dark stragglers
to glory.
        Spending his force
against soft-bellied rush of musk,
dark turns fair, rain turns fire,
forms dissolve in music.

My pillow won't tell me
...
And it like to die.
                    — Theodore Roethke, "The Apparition"

129

Balm to fissured earth, he shimmers
to his flute, filling the fervid lips
the thighs that spin like bowls
upon a potter's wheel.
Such tricks and turns take milkmaid,
cowherd, flowergirl, goddess all as one
while tender-stepping herons sit and
strut and rock the limpid waters by
the cunning groves of Vrinavan.

The pleasure lakes brim white with lilies
aloes saffron sandalwood when Krishna,
sleek as an otter, teases his way.
His love drives headlong like a spear
through a green tree.
The pliant women swell and fret and foam
like indolent water weeds on stormy seas.
"Tell us your name" they beg,
trying to recall his face —

Vishnu naps and multiplies.
He has a million million years to go.

Lord of the wheel has shattered shame
in myriad shapes.

He smiles to think how once
a slippery blue-black boy leaped out of swaddling
into sunlight, becoming fish, wild boar, a million
magic shapes . . .

Silence flowers on his lips.
The temple garlands wink in candlelight,
their musky clusters soaring to
a solitary half-heard flute.

III Siva

Though dancing needs a master, I had none
To teach my toes to listen to my tongue.
But what I learned there, dancing all alone,
Was not the joyless motion of a stone.

— Theodore Roethke, "The Dance"

God-step

Upraised palm

  phat!

two subtle fingers
seeking upper air
and up the high-
curved thigh —

Stone stirs to circling music

cobra shoulder snaking
              round
                      and
      down
              the arm flows
              down a
                      length to fine-
          point
    fingers
                down
      and
              down to
          tapered limb
              to
            rooted
            foot

131

Eternal joy outleaps the
flame-spoked wheel.

Tongue lags and leaden lies
before the lightning miracle of dance.

Healthy and terrible, Siva sifts his memories
like rolling sesame seeds and dancing, sings
a song of hearty tyranny:

"My voice rolls out in thunder claps
forked the lightning of my weapon's flash,
cuts zigzag paths for my far-seeing,
my tongue a breaking wave.

I grind the earth — it rocks.
I rend the earth — it quakes.
Firm as the earth's axis is
my high-arched foot —

it tumbles the mountain buffalo
pounds burial grounds
topples garden coconuts splits
figs like peas —"

Such childish rages!

Ah, they said, *but children only
curl their lotus toes and stamp unseasoned
lie and sprawl exhausted.*
            *Siva knows
what secrets curve a foot
the weight   the measure
height and depth of planting.
Let him sing out his season:*

"I land like a vulture on rocks.
My eye sinks sun and moon

the hooded snake my eyelid,
my slinking tiger-shadow lurks, my mount
a gravid elephant."

New shapes for old! New shapes for old!

"Like dreaming moon in water   or mirage
on the wide spring plain,
nothing is changeless.

Going I stay
Staying I go

My anklets clash I
raise and curve my left haunch
high   higher   higher
   above   the
    rooted
     foot
      and ever round
   the fiery wheel
    turning   turning
      turning."

Dusky powdered human forms
flit shadow-black, blue sapphire-
faceted in fitful spurts of
candleflame
Smoking censers swinging golden
chains linking tiny tinkling bells
surging swinging silken saris
jewelpoints sandalwood   sheen of
musk-oiled hair merging into
   light   stone
    silence

IV Devi

Only Siva, meditating,
could be immovable
in her moving presence.

Tread slow slower
inward and down
soften the loosened
arch lower
lower heavily
down
downward to
smooth softened
sole rising
falling
breathing in
darkness
down —

Ganesha's mother
mother of life
mother of death
sealed in man's
misgivings —

she sanctifies the morning
with her sightless eyes
calm unhaunted

broad rounded haunches
breasts and melon-swollen
belly, heavy thighs
a massive fruitful
cluster...

What sways the soul
is what's invisible.

Light breaks bronzed
over these fecund rounds
flexing around the fluid
girlish waist, curving up
and around, so slender
leaflike chaste, mocking
the dense exuberance
below.

Once a girl, a green thing
quickening, she couldn't guess
beyond the clutch of wind
and flame the rising
falling spiral, bud to
fruit to bursting
back to aching blackness
of infirmity to
ashes, compost.

Once a girl, she sang
without a mouth, high
on a granite mountain —

a floating tenderness
brief as twilight

upraised tendril arms
swaying hips and silver
circling anklets rounding
slender legs drawn
down by beauty's
weight to
earth.

Her water pot of bronze
shining in the setting sun
plumbed wells of deep content,
her parents' borderless kingdom.

Days fell silently like leaves.
Words moved slow as glaciers.

But warring gods and demons pushed
to woo night's daughter,
monster-husbands.

Her bowels turned brass and iron
breasts burst with bitter milk
the rocking thighs imparting
shape pitch weight to mouth
agape —
her eyes drained sorrow's
salty marshes.

O gentle angry mother,
girl that man knows nothing of,
stretched high on a volcano's rim
voicing the tribe's cruel energies:

             a meditating head from Siva
             arms from Vishnu's vigorous fires
             from Brahma's thighs the passionate feet
             from Indra's serpent shape a gliding waist
             the brush-fire of her hair from Yama
             breasts from the ardent moon
             thighs from forked Varuna, all-enveloping
             god of waters   ears shelled from
             the wind's streaming   teeth white
             as curd from the nine Prajapatis
             under a sullen twilight brow
             eyes fish-pools deepening
             into oblation.

Ample water jar
bath of birth   vessel of death
        grain-giver

Lady of milky rain
brooks   streams   fountains
indifferent —

Lady of scorpions   serpents
goose   crowned heron   quail
indifferent —

Lady of bull   goat   wolf   deer
hunting and hunted
indifferent —

griffin   phoenix   sphinx
indifferent —

Lady of caves   tombs   skulls
indifferent —

Gods and men have mothers.
We are her infants slumbering
like sleepy planets
circling endless whiteness —

We suck and turn and
hide our faces.

Footfall

sightless   all-seeing
godhead   cobra-smiling

absence

a lotus opens,
suppliant in
sunlight —

Four Poems from America

I *Father in a Mirror*

In the morning mirror
you are here in me   my eyes
surprised as from our bitter Sundays
cautious, hopeful
silent.

You said, *If it weren't for the Americans...*
while I fought on the other side,
a sullen parody of independence
back in '46.

But Dad, you're here and
I'm the parent now, the shy
explorer taking care and looking
for you at you
in America.

II Southern Spell

The Apopka Blue Darters are coming to play
coming to play, coming to play
by Lake Osceola in spring —

Aloisus and Shad
Sylvie and Tad
Nancie and Tabitha and Quinton and Ziggy
Archello, Idalia, Rocco and Lili
Fleetwood, Cecilia, Wink and Clarissa
Dessie and Ulmo, Tibor and Jitter
Zippa, la Donna, Hub, Thane and Rusty
scamper and nibble by Lake Osceola.

The Apopka Blue Darters are coming to play
The town intellectuals have all run away.

It's a great day!

III *Jack Frost in Florida*

An unexpected place to take his ease.
Will it appease his slow fatigue?

His eyes ablaze with
Oranges   Oranges
more
a hundred
thousand burning in the tracings
of his hourless breath.

He glides upon them
like a storm
clamping their fires out
one by one

his cloaking dream furls
fouls a green-gold world
to brown to
black to

sleep, Jack, sleep.
World, button your coat tight.
Black is white.

IV Band Music for a Grandfather

Why should I fear death today?
My daughter is tooting her bass clarinet
in a real American band.

the high school band
the high school band
the neatest band in this jumping land.
She plays with Chuck and Dwight and Wayne
Elvira and Jimmy and Toby and Jane
and O America salves the pain
as the music soars and roars in the rain.

The space shuttle's up and my spirit's away.
O say can you hear your little one play?
Say, should I fear old death today?
O say

A Tale of the Great Smokies

I Otis Makes a Wheel

I have neither the looks nor the
stature of the immortal gods but
am a human being.

Any kind of hard wood will do, she said
but soon, make it soon.

So I made wheel and hub,
bench and head post of white pine,
spokes of cherry.
The front leg cut from our white poplar
by the well, back legs of maple.

I turned the rounds on a water-lathe,
driven by the stream behind our house,
even with my axe hacked out the dovetail
notch that her thread might
lie easy.

I split the rims from one straight
green white oak and thought my arms
would break. She soothed and urged.
Each day I brought a little of myself
for her approval.

Each end was tapered,
and I drew the split into a circle,
caught the ends together with some pegs.
Then set the wheel up in the attic,
pressed out flat so not to warp it
out of round while curing.

Italicised epigraphs to each section of "A Tale
of the Great Smokies" are taken from E.V. Rieu's
translation of Homer's *Odyssey*.

Soon enough, I said, these things
can't hurry.
Like me she'll come to live with limits
Like me she'll learn what can't be taught.

Somewhere beyond all this drift
the stars are reckoning us up.

2 Penelope Spins

and there she wept for Odysseus

Turn from the word
turn away, he said, schooled in silence.
Made a true wheel, then easy
as breathing, moved down the river
poling his skiff into mist.
           Thin neck
stiffening, set up to catch the winds of this world
in the long hot shaft of our dying summer.

Loving too much, not enough maybe, hardly a
seeker but cheerful. He had his illusions —
we were one of them.
Things went much as usual.
Maybe the stars had a hand in it,
or the one fixed star of my own
grim seeking whose light
blurs my sight like a
drunkard's candle.

Tread air, tread light
silent as dust riding darkness.
Treadle and turn,
black bobbin fat in my fingers.

Soft as moth's breath,
threads slip through tides of my handling,
wordless to wait on his coming,
fixed in my longing for speech.

Compost black currant
fodder horse urine
hickory smoke

          Breath lives,
wavers within.
                              Far below, wide
over the valley burn farmlights
through fog. Dusty signals from
neighbouring hearths.

Tread air, tread light
silent as sleepers in darkness
treadle and turn, unlearn
the bulk of our being, unwind
the tight bobbin. Stand
naked as two spindles saying
in one deep-drawn breath
"I am".

Tread air, tread light
turn again, little wheel.
Darkness has secrets that
light never owns.

3 Uriah Mack Behind the Sassafras

It's either a goddess or a woman.

She doesn't see me. My pulse is a trout
in my wrist.
        The hen tails her string
of yellow chicks with alarm to the barn.

She sleeps in herself like a stone
in the sun, shaping the threads
of his going.

She sings to the air, winding,
unwinding the threads:
"Turn again, turn again
little wheel ever.
He shall have what I am
when he crosses the river."

Neat as a bird in her red headscarf,
loose blonde-greying hair
sun-bleached eyes scanning water.
A distaff of ripe dark wood
pressed close, under her arm
near her breast. Puffball of
rusty black fleece near her shoulder,
spinning the old way.
        Brown fingers plucking
teasing the strands drawn under
to wind the black bobbin as fast
as the wind.

Still centre of everything, sun-worn
like stone, hands leaping
caressing like drunken butterflies
fretting the shuttle.

146

It snags on a
hickory twig at her foot.
Bending to free it, I move.
She backs off, her eyes an unblinking
promise of instant refusal.

There but unseen, suspended to rock
in the wake of her song, I slouch
through the path of her
passionate waiting, scorpion
under a stone.

A daddy's house is nothing
but a cardboard box.

4 Otis Raises Sheep

The fruit never fails nor runs
short, winter and summer alike.

Forty years I tended flocks
on Blue Ridge like my pa before.
We grew the critters just for wool —
a smaller and a hardier strain, no
bigger than your average dog — you
couldn't buy 'em.

Most everybody back
when I was growing up just
kept the ones they wanted.
Stood the cold, the barren times,
never sickened.
Shy and timid too, they ran
in fear from feral beasts,
would let themselves be killed
without a fight. Once caught
and scared, they just gave up.

Most was white but now and then
a black cropped out.
We liked a black born onst
a while. It saved us
from the dyeing.

We shared the extra wool with them
that didn't keep a flock.
Come spring, I fenced the yard and
turned them loose to graze the mountains.
Maybe they'd come back for salt
once a month or so. We didn't take it
to them on account of fearing
that they wouldn't come. You give 'em

salt. Two, three days after they're
gone again.
    All summer long they'd go
a long ways off and stay.

    In fall we'd get out,
hunt 'em up and bring 'em down
through winter.

To tell our own, we notched their ears
on top — Uriah Mack, my neighbour
split the whole ear through
to make a swallow-fork.
I knowed it when we swapped a ram
or two to keep from interbreeding.
We had our marks and knew our own,
but shared.
    Times were the rams would
fight but mostly get along. The
old ones on the mountain had those
long curved horns they'd lock together.
Times were when they'd starve to death
locked in struggle. We found a couple
once, overbit and swallow-fork dusted
with snow, but still we knew the owners.

She wanted to be sure they'd come
down from the mountain in the cold.
I told her often enough they
had to come, just like we do.
    When they want
a thing or two they come. They
wouldn't hardly if they didn't
find a need.

A home don't need no fences.

If anything gets after them

they know to come.
Like us, they want a place at night
to stay, a barn for heavy snows
fine grasses — blue or tender rye —
blades off cane. And voices.

I tell her every time they all come
back. She's only happy once they're
fastened in the barn and feeding.

5 Penelope and the Lambs

the gods had robbed them of their parents,
left them orphaned in their home; and yet
they lived . . .

Spring was always best,
took hold of me like nothing else.

The land's slopes softened green
and graceful right down to
the valley, downward rolled
the children, shook themselves
like little dogs in dotted
fields of lavender.
        Then lambs would
wobble up to suck their ewes
who sniffed and pawed them
into patience.

The old kind nursed their young,
would hold their jug up for 'em,
push the baby to it — either
take it or you die — was in the
tilt.
        No matter what the cold,
they'd clean their babies, dry them
with their mouths, hold breath
right up against them. I'd catch
the puffs of moist warm air hanging
round the little strugglers
in the chill of morning.

There was an orphan once.
I raised it all the way
till it was grown. Then
took it to the barn. It lived.

That beat most things I've
ever seen.

　　　It followed me all through
the house and if I'd get away, it
just stood bleating like my children
when I left a room.

If a mother died, he'd shut the lamb
up with another ewe and force
the feeding on a stranger.

We saved a lot between us,
thinking over.

Spring was always best. To yawn and
stretch and look and love it all.
Even the dark edge
of the distant wood.

My thoughts like little pine cones
float in warmth like feathers,
puffs of milkweed

Dogwood's thick white petals
fretsaw clean against the four black cedars
by the well, the tender push of green
by oak and walnut.
It catches at the heart, almost
like a sorrow I might say
if I didn't know it different.

Roses, phlox and pansies cut a fancy apron
round the yellow house, and everywhere
the smell of wood-smoke, dewberries
the river.

Silenced by joy,
the colour, smell and sound
of everything answer
any question I have
ever asked.

Why talk of time, children, spring
and a river if not to tell
that once we spoke and
listened to each other.

6 Uriah is Hired by Otis

Who knows but we may oust him
from the threshold and the door . . .

Help her when I'm gone
like neighbours do, he said.
She'll need the shearing
come spring and maybe
early fall.

        See that the
well don't dry, the house
stays warm. I ain't been parted
but two days from her before.
I'll pay.

The sun was setting like a big red ball
and yes, I said,
it wouldn't give no trouble
helping out.
There ain't a broken thing
I couldn't fix and
where, I said, my mind
a nest of buzzards, would
you find a dreaming woman
like your own?

I guess a body's like a house
he said, thin and even, but
the spirit keeps on moving.
This time, he said, I'm
putting two and two together.

Seems, I said, like putting
two apart. I don't know
about spirits but this body's

staying put. She won't give me
no trouble. She's smart.
I've watched her spin and weave,
no age on her at all. Most
tenant wives are not the kind
you want around for long, but
yours . . . you're more a fool
than what I ever thought.

He went that summer.
I waited out the winter
till she sent her boy to ask
for shearing in the spring.
If he can help me hold 'em down,
I said, it's twenty head a day
or more, taking the measure
of everything. They're small,
remember; nothing much on legs
or tail — it shouldn't take
but six at most.
Maybe, she said. I'll feed you
give you room and pay like
Otis said. Lady, I said, there's
some around that certain things
mean more to them
than money.
      I asked her what she
thought a man was made for.
She never answered. Called the
hen quick into the barn,
her straggle of yellow chicks
behind her.

    "Turn again, turn again
    little wheel ever"

That song again.
Buzzards hatch in spring too.

7   The Shearing

He'll have your nose and ears off with
his cruel knife, rip away your parts
and give them raw to dogs.

The boy was watching sullen
as I held the first upright,
front legs stiffened
in my grasp.

Cut sure and deep around the neck
the head and down along the
heaving belly
down to hind legs limply splayed
the soft crotch twitching
peeled the curling sheath
off one side. One fat layer.

Just like you skin an animal,
the boy said rigid, pale,
standing aside.

Then fastening the head
between my legs, I shaved
in one fast sweep the
back of neck and shoulder
smoothly down the back
to tail, then down
the shivering flank
in one swift rush
of fattened fleece.

It's like you skinned
a rabbit or a bear, he said again
or something else you wanted bad.
That kid.

She came to gather up the fleece
for washing, filled a metal
tub, hot water and lye soap
and scrubbed. Then laid it
out in heavy swatches to dry
on clean rocks by the stream.
Never spoke a word, not even
to the kid who stood aside
sullen, pale.

I took another sheep between my legs.
Its muscles bunched against my hands.

You have to give them time.

8 *The Dyeing*

And now, as easily as a musician
who knows his lyre strings...

First threads and last.

Smooth thick pale cow-cud
green darkening through oak
past walnut to the pine wood's
distant rim. By now
I know its darkness.

I have dreamed of water.

His flesh was green, the taut
skin of his neck and every
tendon straining out, his face
white against a cold green wall
of water like the stream that
turned his lathe.
It pulled and sucked
swirled mud beneath our feet.

We were suspended so.
Erect in turn, green currents
curling, dimpling round our
naked shoulders in ever-widening
slow dark whorls.

Suddenly I stood against the rush.
It slowed, advanced its tall and
stately waves in a most
sinister silence.
And he was gone.

I didn't know a dream

could be that cold,
its fingers moulding
probing at my bones all day.

The wheel turns.

There's green for birth and spring
in dogwood eye and cedar shoot
and green for death by water.

Unbroken circles loop themselves
tight to the loom's taut warp.
Tension takes time, and
like he used to say, you
can't hurry some things.

Green thread glides from shuttle
feeding from the steady spool.
Weft spins off bobbin
and back in circles
circles...

I washed the plain white wool
in a copper tub. The hired
man started on another ewe,
his mouth like weathered rubber
pursed in silent whistling.

In my tranced discipline
I boiled green oak leaves in a bag
with salt and vinegar for mordant,
strained out the leaves and stems.

A clean unfaltering green.
Wordless.

II

Broadway Vision

And in my dream I saw
a man upon a bus on
Broadway at 100th west.
His jaw pure kangaroo, his
nose both wise and black
and bearing spectacles.

Make haste, O God, deliver me
make haste to help, O Lord

No trousers, underpants with
stripes and limp descending
sox. I prayed to wake as
my straphanging neighbour
pressed against me wise
and black upon the bus.

O hurry, Lord, speed to help
your homesick servant

I sought to move, to leave the
brutish bus. In vain. His way
was forward. He moved speedily
as I backslid. And as he
pressed, I pleaded with the
driver in my uprightness:

Oh help me, Lord, to pray
for words are slow to come

Obey my voice, was what I
would have said but tongue
was locked, confounded.
No voice came. Instead, grey

desperate vapours spread
from nostrils, ears and mouth.

O clear the air, dear God,
release my tongue

Besides, the driver wasn't
wearing trousers either.
How can man trust a bus's
destination when no girdle
cleaves the driver's loins?
You cannot and I didn't.

O Lord, make haste
deliver me conventionally

When suddenly a storm smoked
up the windows, towering
clouds blocked out the light
and hail and thunder split
the sky. I strove in silence
with my beast from whose —

O Lord, I can't believe
this bit —

sharp pants were coming
tongues of flame! A trumpet
voice waxed loud in Aramaic:
"Stop the bus! She wants to
leave!" accompanied by balalaika
in the right-hand corner.

O Lord, my swift deliverance?
my help?

Alarmed, the other passengers
divided like the sea. With

faces harder than the rocks
beneath they cursed my *sansculotte*
assailant who then sank
upon his evil kneecaps.

For the day of democratic wrath
is come. And who shall withstand
your communal pressure, O Lord?

Behold, I am standing at the door
of the bus, and am set down at
116th west in Broadway, NYC
safe from tribulation and untrousered
men with spectacles and
heads of kangaroo.

O blessed Lord, you heard my prayer.
From such tight spots have you delivered
me often enough amid the difficulties
between birth and death. But how much
longer will your patience hold?

And as I sang the praises of my saviour
I looked about me in the busy street
and lo, there hurried men with jaws
like kangaroos, with noses wise and
black and bearing spectacles. No
trousers. Underpants with stripes.

I thought I was awake. It seems you
favour those asleep, O Lord.

The women all had pouches on their
bellies, some with young and all
did flee apace with joyful din in
NYC. Only I had neither pouch
nor child. My name was blotted out.
Awake, I longed for home.

I am much afflicted, Lord.
Let me truthfully remember
what it was to be at home.
Quicken me kindly out of
silence to speak the danger
of being too much oneself.

Bedfellows

*On finding Judith Wright and
John Manifold in* Modern British Poetry
New and Enlarged Edition, Florida, 1984.

What are they doing here,
what are they doing?
Sad and bitter celebrators
of their country's truth:

confusable no longer with Austria
Asturias or Austrât (those films,
that Cup, the eversquawking thornbird)
yet more than water separates
an A from B.

In the tidy wastes of haveagoodwhatever
and yallcomeback, the gorge also
rises to find Manifold bound:
   Tomorrow like another day
   I draw the dole and rust away
       together with
       Pompomes dutiful and bloodless:
   Bored, uninformed, knowing the ghostly silt
   Dispersed, yet tending to this cross of ground.

Nor does it wow me finding
   Look, the whole world burns.
   The ancient kingdom of the fire returns
       sit as kin with
   Why need I fear the bursting bomb
   Or whatsoever death shall come
       in the same old
       double binding.

More than diction parts us here.
To bear the world or not to bear,
but when our time has come and gone
in the shrill kingdom of the dumb,
will we still shrink against a throne?

The Call

for Charles Causley's 70th birthday

hello Charles how are ya
mate remember William
Creek I can't talk
long there's other fellers
waiting and a string of
camels kneeling on the edge
of nowhere and a bloody
great phone box stuck in
the sand like a dunny with
everyone wanting to use
it no poetry's nothing like
life not mine anyway if what
I think a poem is a poem
poets are born not made just
like you said but life does
help eh tell them all to drop
dead I'm talking to a poet
yes it's Australia saltbush
sand and spinifex and 45°
in the shade last week not
Cornwall in the winter eh
the South Australian manager
of Telecom told us it will
change our lives a facility
he called it for what that's
worth Bernie's cranky it's not
hotter they'll do just about
anything for a dogfight here
gets chilly on the Simpson
three dogs and a road train
full of horses for the knackers
in Whyalla and a bunch of
paper men photographers the
blokes who put it in and

tourists looking zonked the
manager unveiled the bloody
thing usually only six of us not
much to see and less to do
bit of a treat really otherwise
we wouldn't get to see each other
all that often spotted nearly
sixty all in all here today and
gone tomorrow plus the manager
that young stuffed shirt a
trendy wouldn't touch the amber fluid
wanted wine facility this
facility that me camel's got his
nose in piss off you whiffy bastard
not you old mate I'll write a
proper letter later none of
this microwave stuff with
pips to stop congratulations
anyway there's a strangler in
a cowboy suit bashing down the
door and me camel's dropped
his bundle see ya

Casting the Die

Only Joseph Brodsky would be daft enough,
Only *The Times Lit. Supp.* could print this stuff,
(or the *New York Review of Books*, a friend of Auden
after all, reputably dissident):

"The poet, the loved one and the Muse" proclaims the
    heaven-sent
gospel: only men write poetry of love, woman can't be other
than love object, muse, or, if she's suitably adroit, a mother.
She may write poetry herself, but by a whisker.
She doesn't match the masculine paradigm, the apparatus
    of desire
can only frisk her,
never penetrate the depths. Nor can she turn a verse to
    potent thrust
and melt of sexual conquest, her ineffectual trust
in smaller things debars her from the Brodsky canon.
She's jealous, callous, hopeless. This is 1990. More anon:

O my hornbill husband, you have a bad smell,
and when Kaaeko comes and smells you
he will take you to Panirai and your spirit
will enter a pig. So runs a Buin wife's lament
for her spouse, lost from view.

Expressing love takes unfamiliar tracks, the ironing-board,
the kitchen sink, the loo:

With a hot glide up, then down, his shirts
I ironed out my father's back, cramped
and worried with work.

Or

Sometimes, shaping bread or scraping
spuds for supper, I have stood in the kitchen,
transfixed by what I'd call love
if love were a whiff, a wanting for no
particular lover,
no child, or baby or creature.

The object of desire may be arachnid,
sprawled behind the toilet door, splayed on a leaf:

I have left you four flies.
Three are in the freezer near the beef,
the other one is wrapped in Christmas paper
tied, I think, with reefer knot
in pink.

There's love, as an arachnophobe can vouch,
more diverse than mere lusting on a couch.

So what does Brodsky think male poets want?
The vacant leaves his mind's imprint bear out.
Male poets seek, he gargles, *visually aleatoric blondes*
over the excessive precision of brunettes.

So that's it. Aleatoric pets.
Aghast, I look it up.
Unpredictable, it says, dependent on
the dice's throw, the dyer's cast,
from Latin "aleator" meaning gamble.

That cuts me out who nightly amble
scarps of lateral thought with makers of
bi-lateral agreements.
Does this mean non-Caucasians needn't apply
to be commemorated in those deathless odes and sonnets?
If hairs be wires, black wires grow on their heads,
and in their hearts, laid neatly end-to-end beneath their
bonnets
if Brodsky be believed.

Dark or fair, if they have wits, do know that love is short,
forgetting long.
That never blocked a poet from a song,
whether in greed and haste they do infect and curse
each other like Robert Graves and Laura, Sylvia and Ted.
Or worse, display their verse for all to read with dread.
Although we're told that literature's not life,
there are more ways to kill than with a knife.

Queen of ingratitude, to my dying day,
You shall be punished with a deathless crown
For your dark head, resist it how you may.

So, if you live, dark ladies, remembered not to be,
Die blonde, or else your image dies with thee.

Primal Dreamcake

What a night and they keep saying
nothing happens in Tasmania!

Just stopped watching this uplifting
bit of Whitman, oceanic swell
gratitude for life even for the humblest
creature down to Walt's noiseless patient

spider, containing multitudes
at one with creation acknowledging the perfect
fitness and equanimity of — God, there's a
spider on the toilet roll, patient,
hasn't moved for twenty seconds.

Trembling in the doorway bladder
bursting but I can't go in I can't
move anywhere I have to keep my eye
on him.

He might shimmy under the seat
lower himself into the laundry basket
fold his hairyness in the tissues
lurk among the pegs
all legs or spin himself
king-size in the twin-tub.

Love of life's draining out o stevedores
brakemen and blacksmiths where are you now?

I'm not enamored of men, Walt, can't eat
and sleep with them week in week out one would be
particularly welcome now I can't sleep
with the spider in the bathroom.

Let it put its ductile anchor someplace else
mark its little isolated promontory
stalking someone else's loo a conservationist
a greenie must be oodles in Tasmania why
pick me meanwhile the spider's nipped inside
the cardboard roll one hairy leg waves out
I tell him in a strangled voice stay there
you bastard wait till I get back and
run the lights are on next door
I knock a woman says she's got no spray
and no she won't come out and no she
can't do anything her door stays shut
the slut I've given up on sisterhood.

Two legs waving now, a friend swims into mind
she lives close by I phone she'll come
a pal at nearly midnight reads her Whitman
knows the Bible backwards comes from Queensland.

She arrives bearing like the grail a green
cloth enfolds the roll with reverence bears out
the nightmare lets it loose at the street
corner purring Lovely baby and she wanted to
kill you did she

To sleep perchance to browse Fay Weldon's latest
blast against wet English flute jobs piping
Pergolesi news about Jelalabad polluted rivers
and dreaming soon a woman with pale eyes pale
hair those marvellous British bones who has
to be Venetia or Antonia competitive about
her children smug in Ladybirds who play
the flute the harp the violin
and probably the dulcimer who doesn't want
to hear about my children whose baby photos
I can't find whose beauty I can never
forget I'm trying to make a school lunch
for my daughter but there's no food she

174

doesn't want to eat and milk is spilling
out from strange places puddles of white
glop keep spreading   spreading —
the woman's husband is a pompous bore
prancing on a shoreline in new Guccis
recorder at the ready braying Must you
bring out all those photographs is all this
necessary can't you get rid of her and we
know all there is to know about music come
here Portia and we'll show her who can play
and sing and do such miracles her children
daily do we know much better don't we.

They all sit on a golden cloud and leave.
He'd have to be a Hubert Osmond Cecil
there's no Bill or Jim to back me waking
weak —

would Whitman stay alone in a bathroom
with a spider? Never trust a poet
watch their actions not their speech
before you go to bed observe the
Ayatollah or anyone who's got a
finger on creation's pulse

Pie in the Sky

for Gwen Harwood

I'm eating an Australian meat pie,
reading a book about
Beethoven's spiritual development.

It's very quiet in Hobart over Easter.
They're all in church.
The pubs are closed.
I've struck it lucky at the deli:
he's Greek.
Life doesn't stop because you're orthodox.

Only connect, said someone bent
on probing creativity's mystery.

I'm only reading casually so —
No excuses, please — a voice bullies me
to order: you're a poet, aren't you?
Try connecting.

And so I do. Try, that is,
twitching the mind's slack elbow.

The pie's distracting, succulent
rich and brown, so unabashed.
It's what it is.

I tell myself no faculty
was ever sharpened on a pie,
no complacency ever flattened either.

Leave it there.
Let the connections connect without you.
I say this to the one who's eating.

The pie is a synthetic whole,
ripe sonata of crust and meat and crust
baked to rule.

No mice.
No rubber bands.
It's 1989.
Three neat movements, there it stands.
Don't think.
Keep eating.

I pour red sauce to break the synthesis,
tomato scherzo.
Joy to balance melancholy.
The season needs a lift.
Four movements now.

Ordinary experience outwits
your analogues with other arts.

Imagine looking at a painting:
a pie is on a table, nothing more.
Acrylic on canvas, neat as pie,
Hockney maybe.

He'd call it *Pie on a Table*.
If he painted himself eating it
he'd call it *Man Eating a Pie*.

He wouldn't call it *Self-Portrait, Nurture* or
The Last Supper which might smack of
egotistical sublimity, claim spiritual
aspiration or a literary humour.
These do not exist.
And if they do, they're only a
projection of our needs.

Needs are for children.
This is adult viewing.

If Andy Warhol took it on
there would be fifty in rows of ten.
50 Meat Pies he'd call it.
Titles aren't the artist's bag.
Still Death would do as well
but never mind — the pudding's
proof enough...

It fastens bluntly on your retina,
leaves your spiritual well-being high
and dry, our gold-brown flaky
high-rise pie humped with flocklets
of tomato sauce.
That's art enough.

It's not:

Little Jack Horner's individualistic self-
congratulatory pie,

or the king's hierarchic banquet, beaky
with blackbirds,

or the tragic moussaka of Thyestes
brimming with his children's gristle.

It is:

an Australian pie
legitimate ingredients
approved by Public Health,
no fancy foreign stuff —
we're Fury-friendly here.

Connections are taking care of themselves.
Our juices flow. Steam rises,
ribboning wisps in air.

In music, it wouldn't match
the *Grosse Fuge*, great C sharp,
nor the *Quartet in F* he polished off
at Gneixendorf: "the name sounds like
the breaking of an axletree," he muttered,
inner ear reverberant with connections.

"Muss es sein?
Es muss sein!"
Simple as pie, we say.

What is it then that *is*?
The pie steams open from its crusted skirts,
red gobbets sink below the rim.

If I were marrying music to this pie
I'd tie it to a wheezing barrel organ
from some innocent old carousel.

A crowd is gathering, nodding to
"The Road to Gundagai" and "Come Back to Sorrento".
Round and round the horses roll
their diamond eyes, stiffening
in full stride, biting the air
with wooden teeth,
letting it go at that.

For A.D. Hope

On the occasion of his 80th birthday

Past the open window
a sparrow flies, dips,

shuts its wings, drops
a little, spreads again

to lift   lift
catch itself rising.

Once, nervous, practically
invisible, I dipped into

your sight, pardoned
for whatever it was I wasn't.

Your dreaming head, freckled
delicate as a sparrow's egg,

charted the contours of
a shaky flight.

The lines seemed clear enough,
the hunters far away.

Kindness steadied the uncertain air.

I wrote a poem about you.
An anthologist thought it was about God.
A critical sleuth hinted at an absent father.

Forgiven still, the mind, listening,
catches a feathered rush of memory —

a little air
a clear pane
and a small bird
falling

Growing Up

When I grow up (I'm only fifty-five)
I want to be as mountainous and wise
as Marguerite Yourcenaar.
A big stone sphinx
silent as a shadow.
The perfect balance between
grace and power.

I want to be strong enough to live
on an island off the coast of Maine,
let my beautiful garden run to seed,
receive an interviewer from some
prestigious TV arts programme
once every twenty years, descend
to read aloud with detached hauteur
prophetic passages from past work,
refuse the academy's accolades.

I will not miss my native land.
I'll know who I am.
My voice will be low, steady,
unemphatic, purged of need.
I will not mind being big-boned,
heavy. I will not notice
that my hair is thin,
that my eyes have come to a standstill,
that earnest questions stay unanswered.
The loss of lovers, children's defections
will leave me cold.

I will become the absolute
it's taken me a lifetime to annihilate.

Reading a Letter in Amsterdam

Under chestnut clusters looped in light,
a firm clean-painted bench.
I'm remembering you as you were before
we met, before I sat here with your letter,
waiting, watching children, joggers, lovers
pass, a blurred and broken line.

You've been away a long time
through all our pointless winters.
I've found you now in tenderness
like something lost in childhood,
remembering you as you were before
we met again, before I sat here waiting
on a bench in Amsterdam.

Like distant ghosts, older men and women
slowly pass the bench in silence. I watch unseeing
what's closer to me now than you,
remembering you as you were before,
as you might be now,
before your bright green spring
cut short our winter,
swam us into flower.

Your voice, a longing subterranean stream
has shaped our story, and your words,
those *words*, shake out like rain
in my cupped hands.

You are not with me.
I've come a long way to tell you
this reminds me of some other time,
some other place, but not the same
as what was lost in childhood.

Your letter's shaking in my green-veined hand.
I open it. Not open —
tear is closer to the truth, my hand
still trembling on a firm clean-painted bench
in sun-struck Amsterdam.

The Ballad of the Pretty Young Wife

for Helen Adam

Here is a tale of sorrow and woe
That happened in time so long ago.
An old man nearing the end of his life
Took to his heart a pretty young wife.

A wife to look after his house by the sea
His house forsaken and solitary
By waters dark, perturbed and cold,
The lair of creatures cruel and bold.

Through murky waves the sharks cut light
She heard their path in the dead of night.
She heard them gather, though far away,
And her will moved with them in search of prey.

"Be still, my dear, be still and sleep
Though the waters are dark and the waves run deep.
My little bride, there's no need to dread
The path of the shark in our sheltered bed."

They hunger when only the easterly howls
Those starving sharks with their harrowing jowls
But when old age sags in a sleep profound
The cleaving fins make the only sound.

She dreamt that she swam in the rising wave
Naked and proud and young and brave,
She feared no sound, she scorned the dark,
Pursuing with joy the song of the shark.

Her fettered soul to its own kind sped
As she cleaved the waters dark and dread.
She breasted the waters so cruel and proud
At one with the sharks she sang aloud:

"I'm free at last to seek my good
I lust for my kind and for human food
And I hate the old man near the end of his life
Who welcomed me in as his pretty young wife."

She dreamt next night of a knife-like fin
And the world opened up and took her in,
And she sliced through its waves like her kin, the shark,
And she lashed her tail when the moon turned dark.

"Show me the path on my quest for food.
Show me the source of life-giving blood."
The moon came out from behind a cloud
And shone with force on the old man bowed

In the bed where he treasured the pretty young wife
The source of his joy, the jewel of his life.
She cries to the moon by the waters cold
As she turns in its light from the husband old:

"How can I yield to a husband's will
When the blood runs free and the sharks smell kill?"
But the moon turns dark and the clouds rush past
And the lives of the two are ebbing fast.

The very next night she climbs to bed.
The moon has vanished. She lifts her head.
"Are you coming, my wife, are you coming to sleep?"
"Yes, I'm coming. The stairs are so dark and so steep."

He turns to his wife lying still in the dark
From her blazing blue eyes flashes out a hot spark
Like a streak of hell's flame. He lies still as death
As she tosses and turns with her ravenous breath.

She pitches him down as his cries float to sea
"Alas for the monster my bed has set free!"
Tonight she is dreamless. Forever is he,
No longer she'll hunt with the packs of the sea.

For the pretty young wife has discovered her prey
In the arms of an old man who hastened the day
Of his sorrow and woe and the end of his life
When he took in his folly a pretty young wife.

Domestic Architecture

The Wife

A rotary hoist in the front garden
and he's an architect. She's glad
he's rarely home, has even learnt to pardon
a plaster Atlas staggering sad

under a crushing ball among the ferns.
She founders over broken toys,
a rusted cycle in the grass, and yearns
for order. They are childless. It annoys

the neighbours when she nightly sings
  'O neighbours, neighbours, I am growing old.
  My husband built a house and gave me rings.
  The house is dark, my child within grows cold...'

The Architect

She always wanted it, that line.
Against my will I put it in
to please her. Things were fine
till Mum gave us that statue. Always thin,

I couldn't bear the load. I stayed out late,
came home to find her tripping and falling
in grass I couldn't tend. My mate
was heard crying and angrily calling

about some child and a house. We had
no kids. I really don't know why
she made a fuss and it's too bad
to think the neighbours heard the cry...

The Neighbours

We don't know why
our neighbours cry...

Jacques Tati at the Darwin Hotel

Bonjour, words! Tell me where I am —
A thousand miles from everywhere,
they say.

Palm-fringed patio
a buzz of mauve, cerise,
pink and gold and green,
cascades of luminous bougainvillea,
frangipani fretworking
a weightless turquoise sky.

Mangoes drop their headlong smoothness
down the ropy vines, arched mangrove roots,
tangibles unlimited.

"Minimum dress for this area will be
SHIRTS, SHORTS, SHOES, LONG SOCKS"

The trustful waitress leaves me juggling
tiny plastic rectangles of butter,
marmalade, honey. I ferret clumsily
around the toast.

And there's the coast!

Improbable tall palms
a still metallic sea
and miles of sky.

People going out and coming in.
A boy is sweeping slowly up the path.

Here's a man with sideburns
short and chunky in his long white socks.
Determined.

He's carrying two large cases out.
The path is long, the greenery too frivolous.

And there's his wife. Her back is young and white
but she's not young. She limps to take a frontal shot.
They have to leave.

Her husband makes his second savage trip,
puts down the bags to help her with the light.
The boy is sweeping slowly.

It's hard so far away and she's unsure just where
the meter is. He shows her.
She snaps and snaps again. She's sorry
there's a satyr in the shrubbery
eating toast.

It won't be like the travel posters say.
But after all, a holiday's
a holiday.

Marius in Hobart, 1989

for Rosemary Dobson

Last night I saw an old French film.
A story told in black and white
about a woman's sacrifice for love.

Fanny, the little winkle girl
with shingled hair, gave up her
hope of cosy domesticity,
releasing Marius to his
South Sea island dreams.

It seemed both right and proper
back in Melbourne's old Savoy in the early 50s
before the soul's innocence was ironed out
that men fulfil their dreams
that women wait without hope
that magic sailing ships should come
and go.

Around the gentle pair clucked
hummed and growled a clutch of comic citizens
whose operatic gestures, male worldliness
about premarital sex we used to label
"French".
Always shaping up and backing off.
No broken jaws, smashed skulls
or knives in backs. Only playing at it.
That was our world.

Rejected suitors took it in their stride,
never reached for guns,
got shrunk on couches.
Absurdly waddling Panisse
a defrocked Alf Garnett with pointed shoes,
enormous bum, retreated graciously

saw through his folly, growing
out of it, a momentary hero.
We breathed again for Fanny.

The men were fat and comfortable
in cummerbunds and aprons.
Enormous-bosomed women in respectable
black satin, no taint of sin upon its sheen.
All wore funny hats, drank wine at midday,
talking, joking on the generous pavements,
light airs teasing the loosened sails
in a peaceful harbour.

A rakish boater for young Marius,
abortive high-crowned Panama for the provincial
Lyonnais whose weedy moustache, fastidious lips
and twitching nose set him up for ragging.
Presiding over all, benign, absurdly tolerant,
sad-faced Raimu played Césare,
the widowed father.

We all wanted such a parent.
We thought they existed in France.
We believed in the forgiveness of sins.
There seemed to be plenty around.

But Melbourne wasn't Marseilles.
Sinister cranes
crouched over iron-grey warehouse walls.
The streets were empty.
The Savoy wasn't France either.
Other South Sea island tests
have taken place and a ship exploded
somewhere in a peaceful harbour.
Somebody else's.

So when I saw this old French film last night
I couldn't look.

The iron gates have shut.
It's too late to say you want to go back,
too late to say you've forgotten something.
You know you'd be lying.

New Age

There's a man on the radio.
He's being interviewed by a woman
with a thin holy voice.
Her name is Caroline. She's impressed.
The programme's called
"The Search for Meaning".
He's impressed himself.
Between the slabs of self-
improvement vibrate slow harp
pluckings, 30s jazz.
He weaves a hairball round TECHNOLOGY.
She feels improved. Music helps
the ball go down.
"What was it like in gaol?" she breathes.
"Wonderful! It brought the holy monk
out in me!" He's ecstatic.
He tells her (twice) he grew
a beard. Goes on to say the beard
upset the governor of the gaol.
"No man in my gaol has a beard!" he roars
theatrically mimicking the governor's rage.
He has observed himself growing a beard
and found it good.
The interviewer ends her business
with a "Peace Be With You".
You can have him for $12 on cassette
at home.

You never know who's waiting for a spot,
dying to keep you quiet.

Miss Short Instructs Her Latin Class on the Fountains of Nepenthe, 1912

...Sparrowhawk
Steiner
Terribile
Titmus and, oh dear,
St Quintin, all here
and unperplexed.

Yes, the guide has just eaten
a raw crab *tremolo agitato*
but never mind; *la volonta di Dio*
and all that. We'll have a drink
soon and yes, Steiner, the rock
is indeed volcanic but the
mount quiescent.

Twelve fountains once,
according to Perelli —
some up high from
inhospitable rocky lips,
others jetting out from
vineyards, orchards
in the middle distance.
The rest near sea and shore.

Ancient healers praised them —
yes, in Latin, Titmus. Maybe
not like science as some
know it but empirical
empirical...
Good enough for Galen and
please, Terribile, put away
that frog. Providence supplies
no useless gifts, I know, but

we are not at home, however
evil-smelling. Restrain yourselves.
I know Greece was home to moderation
but is it too much to ask, Sparrowhawk,
that folly not be added to irreverence?

Faced by phenomena that seem
to mock the rational,
be humble, Titmus. Yes, it *is*
the Mediterranean. The guide
is quite all right...

Saint Calogero's fountain's what
he said and good for gout,
child-bearing, leprosy and,
if you don't eat lentils,
flatulence. Only sunburn,
Steiner. Your mother ought to
know that leprosy's extinct.
Varicose veins aren't your problem
yet, but ancients had them too.
Scorpion stings and other venomous
beasts — do watch your feet,
Terribile. The snakes are harmless.
I promised that I'd bring
you home alive...

The Paradise fountain is
nitrous, Titmus. For distemper.
Farmers fattened up their pigs
and kept them glossy. No,
Sparrowhawk, the Odyssey
took place in Greece. This
happens to be Italy.

Hercules's Fountain proved to
be a laxative, tartaric and
could fix a harelip

vertigo and chilblains,
also a relief from piles the
universally misspelt
haemorrhoids — I see no
contradiction, Titmus.
No, *please*, Titmus, not
just now. I'm sure a little patience...

This fountain known as
la Salina, mostly used
by women for unspecified
complaints. I said
unspecified and meant
it. Recommended also as
a sheep-dip. Let me finish,
Sparrowhawk. The Fountain
of the Virgin — what's so
funny now, St Quintin?

Purgative and blastopeptic,
gave relief from herpes
elephantiasis and
everything of atrabilious
lunatic disposition...

Another which we won't pursue
today relieved the Babylonian
itch and other crudities,
fantastic visions, colic,
and affections of the heart
with which some of
you may later be
afflicted. I strongly doubt
that procrastinating
cataplasia was a raging
plague but you may
have something, Steiner.

The guide has told me
of another which, by
virtue of its smell alone
raised from the dead a
certain Anna Pasta lying
in her coffin. It wouldn't
even wake you up,
St Quintin, but try
to look intelligent...

The Fountain of Saint Elias
soothes all who suffer
lechery and ingrown
toenails and no, Terribile,
please keep your
shoes on. It was never
dedicated to Priapic rites
no matter what you may
have thought you read.
The text was probably
corrupt...

Grazie, the boat *per amore
di Dio*. Why should not a
fountain, Titmus, dry up
if it pleases?

III

Hospice Training

To get there, first you have to pass
the barriers of speech, unlearn
your hard-won plainness.

Is it worth it?

Pass a fence of iron spikes
raised to tear and gut what's crouched behind,
what's dying to get out.

Will it funk the course?
Will it survive?
Will it be free?

Open your eyes.
Try to look as if you're listening.
They're big on empathy here,
dull with concern for the terminally-ill.

I'm feeling murderous,
listening to the air explode
before their words put out the light.

I'm sorry but this is how it is.

When Lucia, Joyce's agonised daughter
heard about her father's death, she said:
"What is he doing under the ground, that idiot?
When will he decide to come out?
He's watching us all the time."

That doesn't sound insane to me.
If you were ever a writer's child
you'd know the terror of a word
from the mouth of a primary carer.

They put her in,
these masters of language,
breakers of the whys and hows of a tale,
deciders of your fitness for the road,
who tell you how to mourn
and how to die.

But concentrate.
Try and forget the words.

Something delicate's alive behind the spikes.
Fix your eye low on that shuddering wing.

It has to be worth it.

Breathing Exercises

Have you ever tried to give your mother breath?

You stand, back to the wall,
a prisoner awaiting execution.

A bad start in life, you might say.
But whose?
We're not talking childbirth.

Desolation keeps you both in check,
as formal as white airless brides.

Her hands undo you, moving in
a slow blind caress,
arching over the clinical sheet
scrunched high in pain.

All you want to do is breathe
the panting mouth alive.
All you want to say, your chances
of being heard saying it,
left the airless room years ago.

Embarrassing scenes in enclosed spaces
were never permitted.

Gagged, you can't move.
Sentence has been passed
without words.

There are no bonds for good behaviour.

Afloat

I knew a father once
who when I said "I want to fly a kite"
became for me a child again,
pretending not to know.

His fingers fumbled with the string
so mine should move more freely,
and everything was airy
blue and light.

In just such ways he taught my arm
a gentle arc in water, laughed me
into dead man's float
and porpoise flip.

Each day I waited for the toy-box
called an Austin
to rumble down the street
between the elms towards a
grey-green Melbourne sea,
jumping the running board
to ride that little strip of freedom
called "our drive" before our mother
collared us to silence:
"Be quiet. Don't disturb your father."

Would it disturb you now
to know I know what duty let you in for?
Or to tell you how, each day,
I wait that day's-end glimpse
of the whispering sea?

Call It Love

They met as prickly children do,
hiding nameless fears.

Their sad ironic faces
promised what they couldn't see.

When he died, she lay awake
an old photo in her head of a boy,
profiled against an apple tree in flower
staring out across the Zürichsee,
infinitely alone.

Curved solid with loss,
his young back shook tears out of her.

All their faltering life she'd hoped
to be a flowering tree for him.

You could call it love.

Reading

NO ALCOHOL: red ink across the page.
Why not, I wonder, hearing again
the social worker's words,
"They've come to die with dignity
so give them what they want."

He's Kavanagh, James Brendan,
steady eyes, fifty-one years old,
a miner from the North, and Irish.
Dependents none.

It's in his lungs.
He sits up straight, alert and shy
his voice smoky as an old song.
"I haven't seen you here before.
You new?"

I've taken Edna's nip next door in 17,
faced Mavis, neck turned tight against the dusk,
who last week chucked her brandy over me
and cried. Both women with no visitors,
children somewhere...

"I'm new and so are you.
Your dinner's on the way."
Eve might have greeted Adam so
in God's fine garden, not too bright
as usual, safe on lower ground.

His sheet reads, Cheerful, independent,
likes to talk.
        The room is bare and clean,
no telly and no flowers,
a monkish radio, a phone.

No books.

"D'you read at all?" I ask who never did much else.
"I've never read a book, but I was fit."
"I'll bet you were," I say, thinking of
pitiless Dampier sand and sun that saps
the blood from a green country man,
loading his breath with dust.

His feet are swollen, stretched translucent,
the white V of his thongs still visible
between the sunburnt toes. I touch them gently,
wandering in the blossoming voice of this
mild solitary man. "D'they hurt?"
"No," he says, 'just the condition. Nothing."

He knows his shape and substance without dread,
one who came and will go quietly
from this cruel country. My reading falls away.

"But let me tell you about yesterday," he says.
I'm listening, Kavanagh, James, no alcohol.

"They took us to a play, just two of us.
I'd never seen one in my life before,
real people just like you and me!
We heard their squeaking shoes,
the floorboards creak. Word-perfect too,
remembered every line. How do they do it?"

O you, who never read a book
or hatched a child or left a wife,
your mother maybe half a world away,
why ask me that, absurd in Eden?

Unfit, I bend to touch his feet.
My hand shakes and he smiles:
"It's nothing. Really nothing.
Just part of the condition."

Home Care

A rented one-room unit
right above the freeway.
Can you spare four hours tomorrow?
Just the usual — drinks, the toilet, company.
Her husband has to get away
to do some business. There's no one else.
They sold their house in Mandurah
to come to Perth. She's having chemo.
Seventy-five, mastectomy and secondaries.
Doing well, considering. One of our nurses
calls at ten. Her name?
How could I have forgotten —
Constance Bryant.

I've never done a home relief care stint before.
The coordinator's tone is flattering.
I'm scared, but I say yes, slow
to knock back chances these days
to apprehend an ancestor.
Anybody's.
Guilt, I think. I let mine slip away
when I was young and deaf
and indestructible.

Bert her husband's an ex-panel beater,
boyish in his seventies, trying
to keep things tidy. His meek front
speaks of order, devotion and
never a harsh word.
What I imagine might have been
had we been different.

He shows me tea bags, crackers,
half a chicken in the fridge.

Her tin of lemonade.
"Maybe she'll eat a bit of nectarine."
"I won't." Her voice comes strong.
"He's only happy when I eat," she says.

Bert's stooped, pink, hesitant,
a mottled moon-faced innocent,
steel-rimmed specs, a checkered shirt.
I'm softening yet again to fall
for the heroic myth, the Happy Family.

Any children? Two.
A son in the army far away,
a daughter on a farm.
They can't get in.
Dad's looking after Mum.

The freeway hums below the balcony.
I'm watching tiny cars slide by in lines
like metal beetles.
Each one has a driver
going somewhere.

"I've brought a rose for you.
The only one alive from last night's easterly."
Bert takes it gingerly, slowly finds a glass.
There's only one to spare.
"Thanks," she says without her teeth.
Air whistles through the inverted U
of a pugnacious mouth, eyes flickering
back and forth.

He finds it hard to leave
worrying his bulk towards the bed
and back towards the door.
She's propped up looking hard at me.
She misses nothing, taking me back
to when my grandmother lived

and died with us, unschooled.
But sharp.
You couldn't fool her with a rose.

A hard life shaped that jaw
jutting above the sheet, a pale
blue nightie with its girlish trim
against the wasted flesh.
"Just show her where things are
and off you go. Give's a kiss."
He does it all, awkward and slow,
finding the going hard.

"I expect he'll go to the dogs
when I'm gone." She suddenly sits up
after the door clicks shut.
Her eyes have sparkled into witchery.
She laughs, grows larger in the bed.
"You see this table?"
Close beside the bed a little wooden stool
stands painted white.
She strokes the surface lightly.

"My son Gary made it for me.
Just a nipper in the primary he was.
We sold up everything. I kept this.
It's mine. Nobody gets it till I go.
I've left it to my daughter. Would you believe
that when I told *him* that
he suddenly got interested. Never was before.
They'll have to fight it out between them."
Then she laughs again.
"I always wanted something of my own.
I grew up in an orphanage. He made it
just for me. My son did that."

I sit beside the bed
but not too close, slipping

in and out of her mind.
I'm wondering how it feels to lie
inside an empty rented box
touching wood, how it feels
to know you're leaving
what might have been, what may be
or what never was.

She tells me that she's getting by.
"Time for a nap," she says.

A mild wind stirs the curtain.

While she sleeps I'll read the weather
forecast, watch the bushfire's pall
above the freeway.
From that smile about her lips I'd say
she's off and dreaming.
About a homecoming maybe,
or just a small surprise for Agamemnon.

Soup and Jelly

"Feed Fred and sit with him
and mind he doesn't walk about.
He falls. Tell him his ute is safe
back home. Thinks someone's pinched it,
peers around the carpark all the time.
His family brought him in it and
he thinks it's gone.
He was a farmer once..."

I take the tray. The ice-cream's almost
melted round the crumbled orange jelly
and the soup's too hot. I know
I'll have to blow on it.

Hunched, trapped behind a tray,
he glances sideways, face as brown
and caverned as the land itself,
long thin lips droop ironic
at the corners, gaunt nose.
The blue and white pyjamas cage
the restless rangy legs.
In and out they go, the feet
in cotton socks feeling for the ground.

"Are you a foreigner?"
"Not exactly. Just a little sunburnt,"
and I put the jelly down. I mustn't feel
a thing: my smile has come unstuck.
I place a paper napkin on his lap. He winces.
"You're a foreigner all right," he says.
"OK," I say. What's one displacement more or less,
wishing I were a hearty flat-faced Fenian
with a perm and nothing doing in the belfry.
Someone like his mother. Or a wife who

spared him the sorrow of himself.
Now he grabs the spoon. "I'll do it."
"Right," I say, "You go ahead. Just ask me
if you want some help." The tone's not right.
I watch the trembling progress of the spoon
for what seems years, paralysed with pity
for his pride.

How does a dark-faced woman give a man called Fred
who cropped a farm and drove a battered ute
a meal of soup and jelly?

Outside the window, clouds are swelling
into growing darkness and there's a man
hard on his knees planting something in the rain.

In Memory, Vincent Buckley

1925–1988

Easy to say yes in winter
to a summer hope, the coming of a friend.

Another chance for two cold characters,
lately warmed, to take death's name in vain,
to laugh and maybe sing.
It seemed a simple thing.

Never exactly personal when young
we stood still, going places slow,
harnessed to whispering ancestors.
Catholic and Jew in a dumb and guileless country,
our heavens and hells were never shapeless.

Two solitudes with clever tongues
enough (we thought) to drown
the clamour of the coming night.
Short on small talk, stoned on
art's austere virginities, frozen in our
private dislocations (that's how you might have put it
once) stalking the metal-rimmed rhetoric
that once could turn a simple word like "life"
to something as seditious as "my body's occasions".

We came to call it 'life", went on to live it
till our passing's halting breath became
too delicate to name.

You taught me Yeats's hardening into truth,
Joyce's defections. Their Dublin meeting flared

213

to life in class. Idealist and saboteur,
rootless high-class Protestant and petty bourgeois rebel
struck it rich for us.

Sometimes the body's occasions take on flesh.
Not rhetoric, but knives that slit the heart.
Nothing time's ironic surgery can't fix.

"I tune my muscles for the strait of death," you said,
writing about the Persians in defeat, with maybe
Ireland's mayhem, murder in your mind.
"Life is a history of absences
And unprepared returns," you said.

We don't know who we are when we are,
whisper the ancestors.
Before there's time to blink away your ignorance,
noble language springs the trap shut, earth tips,
and absence stares us back like dull grey stone.
And on that stone is written: there is no return.

We wouldn't dare to start a sentence now with
"Life is" anything
though gaudy Yevgenis of this world keep talking,
change their coats with every wind,
deform their tongues with dogma, answers for the
taking at their fingers' flick.

You said, 'Some poets are weathercocks, some
weather forecasters. For myself, I want only
to feel Jerusalem's weather."
Surely a yearning mild enough for God
for all His clamour?

If mortality's a blessing, you are blessed,
leaving the song of yourself, the "holy human"
to stretch us, tail you to the sacred city.

"Innocent, cocky, doomed,
Like a conman" — your words, old mate, loving
the ease, the frankness of American speech,
those blessed morsels of the ordinary,
rarer than ornaments of beaten gold and twice as rare
to those intransigent for truth amid imposture.

Occasions of sin
Occasions of virtue
spin into ribbons of air.

We go. All stays the same.

The timid seed pod of the heart
ripens to bursting in creation's fires.
Nothing time's ironic surgery can't fix.
Except a poem.

The past becomes an island of the dead.
Unready, nearly invisible, I swim around
in shrinking circles.

Like birds of benediction taking flight,
your words describe my path,
wedged in the buoyant wind:

"I walk beside these fires because I must,
In pain and trembling, sometimes thanking God
For what they give me, the few poems
That are the holy spaces of my life."

For Jim

1947–1986

I

The minnow class swims in,
plaids and checks of older, innocent America.
Clear-eyed high jinks simmer to a stop.

These are the eighties. Jim is gone
who once sat sassy-tongued in class
learning the meaning of poems.

I'm in his home, alive.
He's dead in mine.
What's a poem now?
Nobody has a dime left to cry.

There he stood in plaid shirt and Afro,
lanky 26-year-old fresh from Ohio State in Western
Australia.
Hello, heart-string!

Have you practised so long to learn to read?
Have you felt so proud to get at the meaning?
What was all thaddabout? he asked, dying.

Shade stunts a crop, squinches a singer's voice.
I want to jump at the sun, he said.
I want to stretch my lip.
I want to be black, he said.
I'm here.

This was the morning of the day of the beginning.

Heading round the bend in the world,
returning to the loved and limber land he left,

I'm in America.
The minnows in my class today are black and white.

Is it because we love that we leave?
Or travel dust around the doorsteps we were born on?

Remember, he said, remember.

Fear not, be candid, said old Walt.
Dwell a while and pass on.
Be copious, temperate, chaste, magnetic.
But pass.

Jim dwelt a while, passed on, branded by unfamiliar light.
Home lacked the bold sunlight he craved.
Home lacked the bold energy he loved.
What is home? Where is love?

Remember with every leaf his coming.

II

After San Francisco, the pilot crackles out the States:
unfurling Nevada, Utah, Colorado, Oklahoma, passionate
peaks and sierras of the west passing,
passing Little Rock, Memphis, Chattanooga, and Atlanta,
passing over endless grasses, shrouded fields
snapped shut in snow
telling the copious tale of love in magic syllables, natural
as breathing: Okonee, Monongahela, Natchez,
Chattahoochee, Oronoco, Homosassa,
Seminole, Osceola, Econlockhatchee, Tuscawilla,
Moccasin Wallow, Slippery Rock, Apopka,
dropping in night down Florida's wrinkled nose
snorting the Gulf stream, the land charged, infused with
magic names, love's litany.

Did Yirrkala, Djankawu, Ngambek,
Mandogalup, Nyuninga, Kondinin
and Wallumburrawang seed Jim's enchantment too?
Sacred morsels of mystery, crumbs of divinity,
red men and black men stirring in their secret places,
dreaming in our yards.

Copious I break sprigs from the tree of death,
copious the yellow-speared grain rising,
copious the question: why?

God talked to himself in the mountains,
stirred from his platform in his secret place:
Folks ain't ready for souls yet.
De clay ain't dry.

And he sang creation's birth,
how seeds of earth and air, water and fluent fire
fused in empty space,
how gases burned, condensed, the land turned hard,

the seas rushed into place, stones took men's shapes
and all the creatures wandered in the hills.

He sang and laughed.
Death took his first taste,
tender grass being sweetest at dewfall.

III

Jim died, casually brushing by an *Eclogue*
while the catheter burst and merciful
morphine swam his head into silence...

Like this clay growing hard, this wax melting soft,
In the same fire may Daphnis feel my love's fierce blaze.
For Daphnis I burn.
Let my spells bring him home.

The minnow class swims in and out.
These are the eighties.
Our feet are set wandering in strange ways.

Got on de train didn't have no fare
But I rode some
Yes I rode some.
Got on de train didn't have no fare
Conductor ast me what I'm doing there
But I rode some
Yes, I rode some.

From Grand Central through the long dark tunnels out
out into highrise sunlight,
out by zigzag fire-escapes spidering the charred and
blackened Bronx,
cratered bombsites, car-hulks black and twisted,
New York's terrible backyard passing,
passing the battered spires, the appalled sky,
passing along the frozen Hudson crossed with strutted steel.
I see two blacks and a dog on the bank.
They pick their way through withered winter grasses,
blackness, wreckage. They stand a moment looking.

Like this clay growing hard, this wax melting soft
. . . Let my spells bring him home.
— This is a rough translation of Virgil's *Eclogue VIII*.

Snow clings to rocks at Spuyten Duyvel, Dobbs Ferry,
Ossining, Croton Harmon, the frozen river leading,
leaden sky darkening in patches, in strange cuts and jags
the ice is breaking up, and clapboard houses sink
beside the riverbank, the ranging hills, shadows of hurrying
tides haunting the river's reaches.

The song is passing, covering the earth, your country.
I am in your homeland, you in mine.
We are no longer innocent.

> *Well, he grabbed me by de collar and he led me to the*
>   *door*
> *But I rode some.*
> *Yes I rode some.*
> *Well, he grabbed me by de collar and he led me to the*
>   *door*
> *He rapped me over de head with a forty-four*
> *But I rode some*
> *Yes I rode some...*

Staving off old death with song,
Twenty-six years old you came.
Forty thousand years old and more you went,
giving in to chance and change, black boy,
rocked to sleep and slumber,
made and unmade by love.

Who put out the lie, supposed to last forever?
Love is when it is.
No more here? Plenty more down the road.
Take you where I'm going?
Hell no! Let every town furnish its own.
Who cares about no train fare?
The railroad track is there, ain't it?
I can jump at the sun, can't I?
I can ride blind, can't I?
I'm black, ain't I?

Darkness.
The brief and infinitely graceful dance of body,
fluid arc of upraised arms,
the dance in air, in empty spaces,
the rush to bite down,
all, all in beauty.

Remember, he said. Remember.

Black child, I will.
I do.

New
and Uncollected Poems

A Small Variant on Intelligence

Somewhere I read that
deeply corrugated brows denote
a limited intelligence.

My brow is furrowed deep.
I thought it was myopic strain in childhood,
memory's cold puzzles, great ideas.

I couldn't see to read.
I couldn't see to see.

But yesterday the ferry drew its length
clean from the wharf's rim out into
a sun-filled harbour and moving slowly out
a smile began to spread my mouth
parting smoothest water furrowed fine as silken thread.
Pure happiness, I thought.

And as I thought the word,
the sunny harbour drenched in light and water
shrank to what the writer
had in mind.

Manly, 1991

Letting Go

Tell the truth of experience
they say they also
say you must let
go learn to let go
let your children
go

and they go
and you stay
letting them go
because you are obedient and
respect everyone's freedom
to go and you stay

and you want to tell the truth
because you are yours truly
its obedient servant
but you can't because
you're feeling what you're not
supposed to feel you have
let them go and go and

you can't say what you feel
because they might read
this poem and feel guilty
and some post-modern hack
will back them up
and make you feel guilty
and stop feeling which is
post-modern and what
you're meant to feel

so you don't write a poem
you line up words in prose

inside a journal trapped
like a scorpion in a locked
drawer to be opened by
your children let go
after lived life and all the time
a great wave bursting
howls and rears and

you have to let go
or you're gone you're
gone gasping you
let go
till the next wave
towers crumbles
shreds you to lace —

When you wake
your spine is twisted
like a sea-bird
inspecting the sky,
stripped by lightning.

Starting Over in Autumn

Halfway wise when young,
who could foresee their stubborn mysteries,
their presumptions of innocence?

They intended to disappoint nobody.
Who could have warned them?
Who would have listened?

Can they imagine today what nobody knows,
the span of a human breath
coming and going?

He thinks she can.
She hopes he might.

And why, you ask, does the poet
(jotting under the broken angel's wing
at the bottom of the garden) sound off
such lamentatory alarms?

Observe the verdant celebrant in his hot suit.
He's not reading the sorrows of Job
unsuited to such modern occasions.
Is there anything you would like me to say?
He has a gold biro rolled behind his ear
for the record, smiles on the dotted line:
hello my friends
we are gathered...

What lasts is what they started with,
the faltering heart and something else.
Nothing won or absolutely lost,
still here imagining a place
where people work and pray and sleep,
the tender rituals of surrender.

Time has changed sides, no longer on theirs.
She almost knows.
He doesn't want to know and doesn't
know he doesn't.

The poet doesn't like those lines.
Forget the poet at the garden's end,
what he knows and can't forget.
He's called today a day like any other.

The earth's still green,
birds hop in the yard in hopeful rain,
the young still wait, gravid with yearning.

Pray for them, their children, and those birds.
Let them attend the grace of candour or whatever
waits behind the soul's clear windows.

I.M. William Hart-Smith

1911–1990

Whatever the reason it wasn't
your poems came first to mind,
those self-denying plants and birds
caught on revelation's edge.
No, it was a sight I can't forget
when long ago you brought the child you were
alive into a bare lecture room in Perth.

Was it Wimbledon or Hammersmith?
Somewhere in London's mean middle classes
you set us down before a timid boy
strangled in stiff collar, bowler hat,
walking reluctantly to school.
The picture stayed with me.
Only Orangemen wear bowler hats today.

The ones who set us free
fly from such tight cages into dangerous air,
how perilous only the timid know.

Easy as a pinhole piercing cardboard,
you took your eye to our strange world
to bring our sight alive.
"Just look. Keep still and let it be,"
said the poems, asking little.

You think it easy?
Try it.

Talking Mermaid

Doing my posthumous glide, I left the amber windows
of the sea, my father's granary all Bible-black. The land
above cerulean in autumn, sun plum in a mist
so beautiful my eyelids prickled like a wounded

child outsmarting tenderness. Below, the plangent
chords, deep-sunk cathedrals tolling benedictions
to the drowned. I felt myself rising through translucent
green high on the wordless surge, once a connoisseur

of loss, stressed syllables and self-reproach,
big for my boots, myopic. Legless now
invisible to love, I'm free to circle silently.
The waterfront is murmurous with attention.

Look, dolphins! cries the waitress to her Sunday
table, Bower Lane corner café. All eyes widen,
blond heads swivel over croissants, oranges and —
there, there, look there! two three four five

dark cleavers barrelling, soft surfers curling high
round shallow turquoise circles laced with foam
to darken, vanish, leap again in light.
No family ever moved more gently.

Close to shore they skim and roll up glistening,
morning's anthem swelling out their wake. In play
no choice, responsibility, vocation. So why
the single human head that bobs and pushes

outward, seeks to join their widening arcs?
They tease and lollop close in chorus file: his path's
presumptuous, chancey, stretching things beyond
his lineage. There is no lyric in the human stride.

See the silent watchers on the promenade leaning
outward to the shining host, the blundering head,
the flash and glide. They stand so still, suspended calm
like innocence hushed before a cortège or a ghosted

hero's speech. The young ones perch like pelicans on rocks,
crane plump over cliff and boulder, hair etched on the wind.
Their hearts are flying with the dolphins, briefly
tender, unashamed, gripped in beauty's stress,

the bobbing head irrelevant, its course imperfect.
Pure play is for the feudal few. I knew a woman in New York,
a man in France, who laughed and dolphins leapt
heaving for the open seas. Were they ever trouble!

She was a cleric's daughter, told my fortune
by the Tarot fraught with wily morose mountain men
afraid of water. Pray for a good death, always the
worry, she added kindly (still her father's child),

calling up planets lightly as you'd pick a daisy.
He was a dreadlocked *colon*, black as bronze in starlight,
slippery coaxer sprouting his burnished hydra heads
to pace each catch of breath. They lit my life,

laid nothing on me but a moment's play.
Pliant now and pruned, I trail a clownish tail,
their secret legacy, across the knives of memory.
Whoever watches creatures of the sea cavorting.

with a happy eye remember those
who made us what we might have been.
Look on this world with underwater eyes, tell
tall tales to the tongueless, take in the hiss

of water-snakes and worms sidling the skull's gape,
cruise the waterfront for song and monkey business.
Learn to breathe on land, feed tears to whales and
forecast, if you can, the grace of dolphin weather.

Push or Knock

It's Monday, fourth of June, exactly two years
since Tiananmen Square, now happily Foundation Day
in W.A. The past lies foggily ahead, small changes
only in one's teeth and verse, a leaking roof.
We're quite grown up in our recession.

Another limbo-long weekend. I fertilise the cumquat,
wonder if the Western Waste truck's working, if
another week will pass before the garbage goes.

A morning visitor arrives: Mr Tang Zhengquiu
from Guangzhou province. He's been at work
translating some Australian lyrics into Cantonese,
would like to question me about my poems.
I see them crucified by surreal consonantal clusters,
smile, and let him in.

He's thin, fine-featured and his coat is worn.
A little jumpy, takes his tea with milk,
just one small spoon of sugar.
His hand is steady, patient, offers me an essay
titled "Sometimes Untranslatable But
In Most Cases Translatable." For me?
How very interesting.

He asks me how I write a poem.
I bring out fourteen crippled drafts of
what's been bugging me for weeks,
a mermaid's monologue, the pages writhing
under blasts and slashes of rejection.
She's legless, going nowhere. He inspects
the murder weapons; victim's done the bunk.

I tell him that the poem's fighting decorative
scrolls, rhetoric's fancy needlework,
the sequinned tale. Does he know what mermaids are?
He says he does.
Seduced by metaphor, I wither into pedagogic prose:
"The lyric voice is struggling with the ordinary,
seams are showing, do you understand?" He does,
he says.

"In China, we say punishing the poem."
His words give off a clang of ancient swords swung
in empty air, slicing through silk.
Are China's teeming millions all so close to poetry,
so tuned to its punitive measures? I'm sceptical.
Art's technicalities have never made our folklore.

He starts some native needlework himself,
tells of a famous Chinese poet stuck for words —
how possible? Then quotes

    The moon shines in the sky.
    The monk pushes the temple door

Should he use "push" or "knock"?

He can't decide. While worrying words around
there comes a great wise bearded seer.
Invited to resolve the matter, plumps for knock
to introduce a little ginger to the sentimental
hush. O yes, I gasp inside,
relieved to choose correctly with the blest.

How fortunate to have a visitor like that,
I say aloud. No sages pass my door in W.A.
We are our own executioners in these wide
free spaces. He smiles apologetically, then asks
if he can snap the poet at work. At work?

If you like, I say, cool as a corner neighbour:
the mermaid coils submissive to the flash.

Leaving the house, Mr Tang chats up the cumquat
blooming on the porch.
"In Guangzhou province we have also
fruits like these in spring. People of Canton
make festival for them."

From Mr Tang I've learnt that
southern China is a happy land, warmer
than the severe, meat-eating north, alive
with vegetables and bearded sages who just happen
to be passing when a poet's in a bind,
a situation in most cases
you could call translatable.

Peminangan

caught
on foot
through the window
of a car moving
slowly up Jalan Dago,
your head high
on a young neck,

caught
on a straight road
between a saunter
and a march,
the disciplined line
of your back
slanted towards hope,

you didn't see
a girl watching you go,
behind glass,
travelling slowly up Dago,
caught by a sudden shaft
of sunlight, bend
towards the pane

Peminangan — "courtship" in Indonesian

Perdjodohan

Set in your father's European suit
wide-lapelled and hairy blue
you seemed so delicate —
I loved you for the courage
in your bones.

I floated loose
in Mrs Pronk van Hoogeveen's
rumpled linen, several sizes past
my own, incongruously remembering
my father's lady on the side
and, casually, how Mrs Pronk looked
something like my mother.
But this was not the time or place
for others.

A trail of moon orchids dangled
down the water-cooler's fins;
my hand was trembling on the stem.
Hold on, you said. *We're off.*

I held you fast, the orchids flew
behind, a knot of scraggled *ayam*
leapt and scattered in our wake,
bombed-out feather dusters clucking
huffs of winded dignity.

I hugged you laughing,
relieved your profiled lip
had twitched into a porpoise curve.

Perdjodohan — "marriage" in Indonesian

Newly married! Newly married!
sang the motor bike to dust
puffs rising from our dash.
We were, and how I wished to be.
Why then do I remember,
thirty five years on and stubbornly
alive, how in Djakarta once
I looked into a mirror,
tying back my hair deliberately
beautiful as any tireless mermaid.

White ribbon just in place when
Mr Pronk van Hoogeveen stepped close
to fasten in upon my eyes
glowing with possession:
You're going to ruin your life he said.
The jasmine-scented air closed in.

I tugged the ribbon tighter
tossing back the tumbling switch.
And leaning to the mirror laughed
like one possessed of something
not yet owned or named.

Kera Kera

Climbing steep to Lembang on the bike
through dusk freed from a day's dank heat,
the cool was sweet on our skin our eyes
and sweet the scented air reverberant
with frogs, gongs. I gave up words, let
go like flights of small dark birds to
match your moth-like silences, my Western
outlines blurring and dissolving,
your dreamer on the dickie seat.

Tea-pickers of Priangan gone,
gone the *kerbaus* shunted stumbling home,
gone the *tukang's* bent-kneed glide,
the bobbing poles, the whacked tin
kettle, coconut shell and drum
dying down to soft night murmurs
laced with burning needlepoints,
the fireflies' swooping nets.

We sat in the teahouse garden
under a tea-rose bower to let
the lower world cool off. Far down the terraced scrawls
thin films of mist filtered the dying light
into blue-mauve evening. An old black Gibbon
kept an eye on us, our *air djuruk* thick with sugar.
Loose in a jumping crouch, swinging skinny arms
he hung about for what a human means
by time's rewards.

Kera — Indonesian for monkey
Kerbau — bullock
Tukang — peddler
Air duruk — orange juice

It grew dark fast. Black clouds blossomed high
over the Prahu rimmed by sunset's sizzling
orange fuse. I saw those running bursts, can
see them now alive in no particular order
alive in no special way alive
remembering how you used to say
it was getting to be time
to drink up and come home.

Akibat

I said I can't imagine life without you
as the coconut man passed our window
tapping his shell in the dust

    toc toc   toc toc

I said I'd stay with you forever
as we ate our first meal by the window
(tiny *ayam*, beans and carrots), sunlight pouring in
on the terrazzo floor. The air so still,
the babu's brown feet splayed soft beneath her sarong,
smiles enveloping our joy.

Njonja muda tuan muda, she would chuckle
young Mrs young Mr — how could she know
that we were only children?
At our age she'd given birth to eight.

At night we laughed and rolled on rice grains
pimpling the mattress. She wanted to make sure
we'd have a child, young njonja and young tuan.
Outside the window the kebong's twig broom
whispered over gravel like a blessing

    sh sh   sh sh

You told the story of your ruined childhood
as if it happened to a stranger. I was torn
with pity under the hammer blows.
Ashamed for outliving you, I can't forget,
a long way from that house, that window.

Akibat — "outcome" in Indonesian

More UQP POETRY

Selected & Collected volumes:

Robert Adamson   *Selected Poems 1970-1989*
Bruce Beaver   *New & Selected Poems 1960-1990*
John Blight   *Selected Poems 1939-1990*
Charles Buckmaster   *Collected Poems*
Michael Dransfield   *Collected Poems*
David Malouf   *Poems 1959-89*
Thomas Shapcott   *Selected Poems*
Jennifer Rankin   *Collected Poems*
Judith Rodriguez   *New & Selected Poems*
Andrew Taylor   *Selected Poems 1960-1985*

Susan Afterman   *Rain*
Bruce Beaver   *Charmed Lives*
Joanne Burns   *On a Clear Day*
Gary Catalano   *The Empire of Grass*
Gary Catalano   *Fresh Linen*
Silvana Gardner   *The Devil in Nature*
Roger McDonald   *Airship*
David Malouf   *Neighbours in a Thicket*
Philip Mead   *This River Is in the South*
Dorothy Porter   *Akhenaten*
Dorothy Porter   *Driving Too Fast*
Philip Salom   *Barbecue of the Primitives*
Michael Sariban   *A Formula for Glass*
John A. Scott   *Singles*
Thomas Shapcott   *Begin with Walking*
Thomas Shapcott   *Shabbytown Calendar*
Thomas Shapcott   *Travel Dice*
Peter Skrzynecki   *Immigrant Chronicle*
Bobbi Sykes   *Love Poems & Other Revolutionary Actions*
Andrew Taylor   *Folds in the Map*
Andrew Taylor   *Travelling*
Andrew Taylor   *The Invention of Fire*
John Tranter   *Under Berlin: New Poems 1988*
Dimitris Tsaloumas   *Portrait of a Dog*
Dimitris Tsaloumas   *The Book of Epigrams*
Dimitris Tsaloumas   *Falcon Drinking*
Dimitris Tsaloumas   *The Observatory*
Fay Zwicky   *Ask Me*
Fay Zwicky   *Kaddish & Other Poems*